The Art of Social Influence

ADAM FLORES

The Art of Social Influence
Copyright © 2017 Adam Flores

Disclaimer

Also by Adam Flores

eBook
Turn Your Passion into a Product:
10 Ways to Get Paid for What You Already Know

Online Courses
The Business Club Academy
The Art of Social Influence
Passion to Product

Speech Topics
-The Art Social Influence
- How to Start a Movement
- Pursue Your Passion
- The Driving Force of Innovation and Creativity
- How to Master the Art of Social Selling
-How to Build a Winning Team

Coaching and Training Topics
-How to 10x Your Online Business
- How to Position, Package, and Promote Your Product Online
-How to Master the Art of Social Selling
-Building More than A Brand

Branding and Media
Founder of TheBusinessClubAcademy.com
Founder of DigitalBrandCreatives.com

Adam's Personal Site
Adamimobflores.com

Get the Online Curriculum @ TheArtofSocialInfluence.com

About the Author

Adam Flores is primarily known for his ability to combine the best principles in leadership and social media. He has developed several coaching programs for Entrepreneurs and is the founder of *The Business Club Academy* and Founder of *Digital Brand Creatives.*

At a very young age, Adam has already mentored thousands of people in different parts of the world. He specializes in helping people articulate their message and promote their passion in a way that allows them to make a lucrative income and impact doing what they love. Adam has dedicated his life to serving others. He has launched start-ups, ministries, built sales teams, and helped non-profits share their message through Internet marketing and social media strategies.

Adam believes that leadership skills are the key to developing influence in the social space and in the real world. He has been asked to speak for companies, schools, and universities on this topic. Although Adam serves on a larger platform, he still has a passion for coaching others on an individual basis. He mentors his students on how to have success in business while pursuing their passion.

Adam continues to pour his heart into people. His desire and mission in life is to see others reach their potential by making a living doing what they love, following their dreams, and living life more abundantly.

To book Adam to speak at your next event, visit www.AdamiMobFlores.com. To connect with Adam for coaching and receive free leadership, inspiration, and online business training, visit www.AdamiMobFlores.com.

He looks forward to seeing you on the other side.

Acknowledgements

I want to first start out by thanking God for all of my success. His wisdom and love has poured into my life beyond what I could have ever imagined. It is only through His love – that the Lord has blessed me with wonderful friends and family, and orchestrating relationships with people who have helped me along my journey, which I'm so grateful for!

To my Mom — Thank you for introducing me to personal development from birth it seems… giving me the opportunity to direct my own path and find my purpose. Blessed, is what I am, to have had you show me Agape love at an early age. Our heart to heart conversations have been life changing… giving me the inspiration to think outside the box – and, <u>that</u> has made all the difference! I love you.

To Johnny, Tiffany, and Dave — I love you all. My brother, sister, and Dad have all been a rock of support –listening, encouraging, and loving me throughout this journey.

To the love of my life, Brianna — You are an incredible woman; a beacon of light and inspiration whose love has helped me understand what it means to live life in harmony.

The joy you have in your heart has stretched me to strengthen my relationship with the Lord, and has inspired me to utilize my potential to the fullest. Life wouldn't be the same without you, and I look forward to a beautiful life together! I wouldn't be where I am today if it weren't for you.

To my friend and partner Jay —Your steadfastness and courage to go after a big vision has proven to show great character and determination. It's already an awesome beginning, and can't wait to see what the future holds! Thank you! I also want to thank the rest of my team: Kevin, Alex, Kaitlin, Tony, Victor, and Nick Sandoval. Special thanks to my good friend Marcus for introducing me to online marketing space.

To the first business mentors/personal coaches - Brooks and Ernest — Your insight and direction in the world of business at the age of 18, has allowed me to develop the skills I needed to pursue my goals. Thank you Alex Reynoso, for introducing me to a great opportunity, and delivering on everything you said you would do. Iron sharpens iron, and I will always be grateful for the knowledge all of you have passed on to me.

To the coaches I have had the chance to learn from in person, at seminars and conferences, and in video courses and audio programs. Thank you to Tony Robbins, Brendon Burchard, Eric Thomas, Eric Worre, Ryan Deiss, Frank Kern, Gary Vaynerchuck, John C Maxwell, Simon Sinek, Chris Brady, Orin Woodward, Domingo Silvas III, Chalene Johnson, Jeff Walker, Harvey Mackay, Grant Cardone, Tom Hopkins, Les Brown, James Malinchak, Seth Godin, Dan Charlier, and Christopher Schleoman.

The root of everything in my life has come from God, and to that effect, I am extremely grateful for the people who have filled my life spiritually. Thank you to Joshua Flores, Tom Challan, Pastor Ben Amos, Todd and Anna, Juan Meza, Dave and Dianna Gruber, Pastor Dan Caroll, Joyce Meyer, TD Jakes, Jim Cobrae,

Dan Roth, Pastor Marco Garcia, Diego Mesa, Francis Chan, Andy Stanley, John Bevere, Rachel Hamm, and John C Maxwell.

To everyone else who has invested in my life who I did not mention, I am thankful to everyone who has impacted my life, including all of my friends, family, partners, and supporters. My journey would not be what it is without all of you.

Dedicated

To my Mom, who has always encouraged me to seek God in everything I do. She has been there for me throughout my journey, and I could not have had the perspective and drive I have today if it weren't for her commitment to raising me to be a good, hard-working man.

Note to the Reader

This book is written from the personal experiences of the author. The intention is to provide sound, relevant information that can enhance your business. The ideas and projections shared in this publication are not guaranteed to produce results. The author cannot ensure that the concepts in this book will work for every individual.

In no way is the author rendering accounting, legal, or professional financial advice. The author and publisher of this book are not held liable for any investments made from the ideas and projections of this book. The reader should seek consultation from a professional before making investments or implementing the ideas and examples shared in this book.

Although there is a high level of accuracy and transparency in this publication, there is no guarantee the results you work to obtain will match that of the author and the people who are used as examples in the book. The publisher and author disclaim and release any liability and responsibility for loss, risk, or any damage that may result in an unfavorable circumstance from the direct or indirect application of content in this book.

Table of Contents

Introduction

"Fear can't hold its grasp on someone determined to serve others."

—Adam Flores

In this book, I aim to illustrate the art of leading others through your message and story on social media. Social media has been the great equalizer to those wanting to share their message and gifts with the world. We now have the resources available to bring about great change, impact, and even a great income doing what we love. I believe generating revenue is a major key on this journey as the more resources you have to invest in others, the more people you can serve. I believe now more than ever that the world is looking for people to rise up above the noise in this social space. This book will show you how you can make an impact, lift yourself above the crowd, and create a lucrative income stream through The Art of Social Influence.

This book will focus on three key elements:

- I have something extremely valuable to share with the world.

- I have the ability to impact thousands of lives and I will learn the proven, effective strategies that leaders use to do so.

- I have the ability to multiply profits, increase income in all my endeavors, and start movements through social media.

There is in fact, a way to break through the barrier and connect with the audience who needs and wants what you have to share. Knowing how to share a compelling message through social media has impacted nonprofit organizations to reach more people, helped individuals share their passion with a bigger audience, and impacted businesses immensely.

This book was not written for the person or business that has it all together. I wrote this book to the person or organization that feels they have a message to share with the world and hasn't yet tapped into the full power of marketing their message online.

Do any of these thoughts sound familiar?

Why do I consistently post content and don't get the results other people do?

I feel I have something great to offer people. I just don't know how to stand out in this noisy world.

If I can just learn how to grow a following I could help so many people with what I do.

If any of these thoughts resonate with you, know that you are not alone. So many people feel the same way. The good news is that you are a few shifts away from a big idea that can change it all for you. Before diving into a book filled with ideas to help you grow, I want to focus first on your motives.

Why do you want to grow a following and make a greater impact online?

Here is a tough question that may require your honesty. Is it out of your own selfish ambition? Is it out of your desire to be significant? Is it the power and influence you ultimately desire?

I challenge you to stop for a second and examine your heart and motives.

You may be wondering as to why I would ask you to do this. If you are curious, I'll tell you the truth. Too many people get so focused on the numbers and they often forget that behind every number is a person. That person is intelligent, has feelings, and is really smart. They know whether or not you are genuinely out to help them or if you are just trying to sell them. I've seen too many leaders succumb to dropping their moral compass to do "whatever is converting".

Instead of aiming for just numbers, lets aim to build a following around you, your story, personality, gifts, message, and your authentic-self. It's about growing a following that will be with you on your journey for a lifetime. What you will notice is that converting your following is simple to do when you come from a genuine and authentic place. It's from that place people can receive the value you have to offer them.

I want to make a bold statement now and if you disagree at this point of the book, this reading material may not be for you. If you think you can get online, promote an ad, and expect to build a loyal tribe that loves your cause without providing massive value, you can forget about it. It's the grandest delusion among anyone trying to grow a following in the social space. My desire for you is to have a long-term vision. Be willing to pour out content and be patient. Know your followers will come as they see the value you can truly provide for them. I promise you it is worth it to build your following the right way.

If you haven't heard it before, I'm here to tell you that your motive matters. We are not driven to succeed chasing our own selfish ambitions. We are capable of much more when we are determined to serve others.

Instead of taking on the burden of having to grow a following for the sake of not shrinking to your competition, why don't you think about the problems you can solve and how your ideas, products, and services can change people lives. Metaphorically speaking, I believe something magical happens when your desired impact goes from your head to your heart. When you truly are driven to use your gifts to make an impact, there is a genuine energy that radiates through you. Your audience can feel it, they can feel you, and they will be drawn to your voice, your message and what you have to share with them.

This book will challenge you to take a stand for what you believe in. If you are waiting for the perfect time to start it will never come. In the eye of the camera, it's normal to judge your image, your speech, and body language. You may even question the quality of your content, and contemplate if what you are doing is really going to bring a return on investment. The only way to overcome fears and insecurities is to stay consistent with your actions.

This is your opportunity to fight for your cause and lead people to what you know to be true and right. With any fight you can also expect to see resistance. Don't allow criticism to discourage you along your journey. In a social space where everyone is given a freedom of opinion you may find people who don't agree with your views. Unfortunately, these people may leave unfriendly feedback. Leaders don't engage with these type of responses. Instead, leaders use these responses as fuel to continue their mission dedicated to serving others. In the event you encounter negative chatter, pay it no mind. Overcoming criticism is something every leader must face as they make their mark in the world.

On the other side of criticism is impact. Your content engagement begins to increase among your followers, and your reach begins to grow. Overtime, your inbox notifications begin to rise, and your online presence is getting to be known.

You may think that the possibilities may seem surreal, but in fact they are very attainable. My aim is to teach you how to position yourself as a leader who can lead socially. I want to show you in a way that is simple, reachable, and realistic, so you can take action without hesitation. It would be an injustice if I were to ignore the fact that this could be potentially the scariest thing you ever do. At some point, everyone pursuing impact will experience doubt and fear. Some may feel they lack credibility, some will doubt their ability, and others may question the time and resources it will take to launch something significant in such a daunting social space. Know that it is a process, and that success has an order by which it operates. Also, know that it is impossible to fail if you are leading with something you believe in. In this book, I am going to walk you through, phase by phase, the necessary steps and skills to build your audience. I encourage you to embrace the challenge. The process will be simple but not easy. Just remember one thing: When you realize this journey is not about *you*, but about something greater, you will find new courage and boldness. Fear can't hold its grasp on someone determined to serve others.

Leaders Build a Following Around Their Vision

"Here's the reality: Everybody wants a following, but it's leadership they need."

—Adam Flores

As I consult with organizations, businesses, and individuals, there is one common question: "How do I grow?" In a changing world, the answers are not the same as they once were. Marketing strategies and attempts for massive exposure has only left room for more frustration in this fast paced social space. No sooner have you discovered how to strategize in one area, to find that it is now obsolete in a month and now moving on to the next "big" thing. Entrepreneurs are taking too much time trying to invest in social media and online strategies, only to find a lot of time and money wasted.

Social Media is no longer a new concept, and we have moved far away from the introduction of the Internet. Tech-savvy help is no longer rare to come by or difficult to find. Resources such as apps, blogs, videos, social media platforms, live streaming, and social advertising are now standard practices among anyone trying to get out there and expand their ideas and businesses. What was once new is now a way of life. People are trying to utilize this way of life to gain exposure. However, they often end up frustrated that they are not able to benefit from these resources the way they would like to. So the question is no longer, "Will I use the Internet to grow?" but instead, "How will I use the Internet to grow and be effective?"

I'm not referring to cool strategies on how to post engaging content. I'm talking about starting movements, combining strong leadership principles, and integrating them with social media strategies to promote your cause, organization, or business. Unfortunately, not everyone can pull this off. It requires leadership, the right team in place, and a clear strategy. However, this combination is necessary to standout in a saturated world of marketers, sales people, and entrepreneurs who are all after the audience that you wish to attract for your business and organization.

I want your influence in this space to grow beyond average. Our social world is beyond connected, and I believe that you can penetrate this social atmosphere with unique and valuable content that people really need. This is about making moves and exponentially growing in your endeavor. You will need to take your own journey. However, the ideas in this book will help you with critical principles that will serve as a launch pad for the pursuit and development of your mission.

My desire to become an expert in this field of study was born from my own frustration. I had a burning desire to share my message and attract business utilizing the power of social media. I would watch viral videos like "Charlie Bit My Finger" and "Gangum Style" spread to hundreds of millions of people throughout the world. That frustration continued to fester within me, knowing that I had life-changing solutions—solutions that could make a huge impact—and I couldn't even reach a few people in my circle of friends on Facebook. If I could only figure out how to create a movement online, even a fraction of exposure could change my life and the lives of my potential customers.

I had studied from some of the top Internet marketers across the globe, and I didn't always like their style of marketing. On most occasions, their techniques seem very cheesy and they often bombard potential customers and clients with bad messaging. No one wants to be that annoying marketer. I longed to be someone who provided real value to real people. My heart was rooting for the people with some product or idea of value, and I was stuck watching the world's silliest videos go viral before my eyes. So I made a decision to break past this barrier. I combined the greatest principles from the top leadership gurus with the best strategies from top Internet marketing gurus. By bringing the two fundamental principles together, I was able to start my first movement using social media.

Within a year of starting that movement, my business exploded. Knowing my message and story was getting massive reach even while I was asleep was an amazing feeling. My inbox was flooded with interested potential customers, and I built a community of raving fans. It was a dream that became a reality and there was so much meaning added to my life knowing I had built something that served people beyond what I could do on my own. It felt great being able to break past the wall that held me back for so many years. Today, my sphere of influence is even larger, and I feel even more fulfilled. That initial success enabled me to focus my purpose, and I now consult with ministries, non-profits, and businesses. My passion now is to help others learn about the very principles and strategies that helped me soar in this new era of business and entrepreneurship.

If there were one specific thing I could be proud that I accomplished, it would be that I have mastered a skill-set that I can now share with you in this book. The rewards of implementing the strategies revealed in this book are endless. If you have a business, imagine your brand exposure multiplying exponentially. Not only could you be getting financial results, but you could gain a community of people who want to be involved, who want to contribute, and who want to continue their journey with you. From that loyal community, there is a strong possibility that your supporters will begin to share and promote your brand in their circles of influence. This means you would have built an audience that builds an audience, without ever paying them to promote the very thing for which you are aiming to get exposure. Now imagine the social capital that comes with a thriving organization full of excitement and momentum. In this enthusiastic environment, the culture of your team will change, and the future will shine bright with possibilities. This is a common scenario among organizations and businesses that master this art of social influence.

The reality is that most people are struggling to get results. The majority of people are spinning around in circles, trying to figure out the most effective solutions to grow their audiences quickly, and they are just finding themselves frustrated. Social media has become more like the puzzle that you built as a kid with missing pieces. It only leaves you frustrated, stealing your time, money, and worse, your emotions as you seek the solutions to increase the power and position of your endeavors.

The process of mastering the social space is particularly challenging because it is about understanding people. If you haven't figured it out, people are not as easy to influence on the Internet as they used to be. People have compromised their sleep, resources, and work ethic to crack the code—to figure out how to connect with the most people online. Meanwhile, they are missing the root of the issue!

Many of my students and clients come to me with the same misunderstandings about the Internet. Here's the reality: Everybody wants a large following, but it's leadership they need. If you want to master the art of social leadership, you have to understand people. That is why I could not write a book with only strategies. Strategy without understanding of the psychology will not work in this day and age. Therefore, when I share a social media strategy in this book, I take into consideration the key characteristics of human nature and the timeless principles of leadership.

If social media were just about strategies, then everyone would be successful doing it. You have to learn how to utilize the right skills to lead people to make a decision. That decision may be to buy from you or it may be to follow you. Regardless of the objective, leadership online is necessary for success in today's time.

Now I will admit, there was a time when you could use cheesy marketing techniques and get massive results, but those days are long over. Social media is a way of life now, full of everyone's agendas and thoughts. The people who will survive long term will have to rise above the noise. People are already aggravated that their space and privacy has been invaded with mundane advertisements. However, even though it's a crowded space, I believe there is still a huge opportunity available to build a massive audience that desires to follow you for who you are and what you do.

The world is looking for leaders to step forward. Global communities are looking for people, companies, and organizations to add value into their lives. People are constantly searching for answers, and if you can position yourself correctly, you can set yourself up for massive success. The greater solutions you can provide, the more lives you can change and the greater profits you can make.

How would it add more meaning to your life knowing that you're reaching thousands of people every day? If you have a business, how would it feel to have customers come to you from around the country or around the world? If you have a non-profit, how would it feel to have a community of followers that would like to financially contribute to your cause?

What about your lifestyle? How would it feel to have a flourishing business that produces major profits? How much simpler would your life be if you could create a demand for what you do and not have to constantly chase people who aren't interested in what you have to offer? How convenient would it be to work from your computer and not have to leave the kids behind to get your work done? Working through social media is extremely mobile, and you can even move your work to coffee shops, beach side cafés, or even countries where you travel. In a world so connected, the opportunities for an amazing lifestyle are endless.

Here is the big news: You don't need a lot of people to make a huge impact and generate a large amount of profits in your business or organization. Instead you are simply required to stay relevant and consistent with a plan that produces results. In the past, it might have taken you a lifetime to build your audience. Think about how people used to grow an audience in the old days. They had to have some type of credentials and many years of experience to be a qualified expert in a field of study. That background gave them the credibility they needed for companies to bring them onto their stage so they could share their knowledge with the audience about a given topic. They networked and placed their contacts on a mailing list, and from there, they mailed out their marketing material to allow their audience to learn more about their business. For the people who had deep pockets, they could have developed an infomercial, but most had to do it the traditional direct-mail way. Building a loyal following could take a decade or longer; it's an eternity in comparison to what you can accomplish in a couple years in today's time.

In this day and age, your ability to grow an audience is immeasurable-- you have to be on your game and ready! Your plan has to be more strategic since attention spans are shorter than they ever have been before. People flick through newsfeeds faster than they can read, and their eyes glance over the screen until something catches their attention. Who knows what they are looking at? They may be viewing a live stream of their friends late night out, a picture of a friends holiday gathering, or got your attention with a video showing you someone's dog that spins in circles chasing its tail.

Even the most talented people with amazing stories are having a hard time getting their message out there in a big way. Not to mention many marketers are having a difficult time connecting with their targeted audience too. The majority of the marketers release so much content now that they are having a hard time releasing content of value. Instead, they often put bold red lines around their pictures with red arrows pointing to the action button or they beg you to watch their live channel so you can see their free giveaway. People just don't care about awesome deals anymore, because everything is an awesome deal nowadays. So we continue to scroll down the rest of the newsfeed until we get what we want.

When I say you need to bring leadership principles online, it's about getting people what they want, in a style they want, while still communicating your message. This could even be releasing content as entertainment, inspiration, or a video that creatively serves as education. Leadership in the social space is about understanding what grabs people's attention while still adding value to their lives. It is about knowing what you stand for, and releasing content in a way that is relevant to your audience. People will hardly remember the content you released, but they will remember how they felt when they viewed it. It is about packaging value to create an experience. By using your content to create an experience for your followers, their subconscious mind won't throw you out the window the next time they see your post. It's important to identify the style and delivery that works best for you and to continuously serve your audience with that type of value.

You Are Needed By Others

Over the past seven years, I've had the chance to sit down with over two thousand people over a cup of coffee and converse about their dreams and ideas. On the surface, I have observed that we all have our own needs and ambitions regarding what we would like to accomplish and the lifestyle we would like to live. However, at the root of who we are, there is a desire within us to do something great in order to serve others and make a difference.

Whether you are at the surface stage, or whether you have found the deeper meaning of what you are called to do in this life, every vision requires the ability to learn and understand people. With people, our visions have meaning and can become masterpieces, and without people, our ideas and innovations are meaningless. Becoming a social leader is necessary to build an audience around what you do. I believe it is one of the single most important skills you can develop in today's time.

The journey begins with you. I encourage you to clearly establish who you are and what you want to give to the world. Are you passionate about a message, product, opportunity, service, or business plan? Whatever passion you may have, there is a story behind "why" you are passionate about it. It's the "why you do what you do" that draws people into your vision. To add onto the latter, it's the realization of "why others need you" that will give you the drive to keep serving others. How can you package what you know and why you do it so that you can bring uniqueness and authenticity to the market place? You are so needed by others!

I'm here to urge you to never doubt the burning desire that is within you. Do not ignore that tug on your heart that pulls you to give back and do something fulfilling. What makes you unique and different is "your" story. Believe that the product, vision, mission, or service you have to offer is valuable and someone's future depends on finding what you've discovered. The world tends to wait on the next leader to rise up. Why sit back and wait? If it isn't you, then who will it be? Don't be intimidated by others and don't be intimidated by what is "required" to be successful. In fact, building a massive business through social media is actually quite simple. Believing you can do it is the hard part.

Your Struggle is Your Victory

Now, I hope you don't think my own journey was a rainbow with a pot of gold at the end. For many years, it was just rain. I remember working as a dishwasher at a golf course. I worked in the restaurant on the second story of the clubhouse. It had huge glass windows that overlooked the course, and I would see golfers playing in the middle of the day. I always thought to myself, *"How do people play golf in the middle of the day?"* I used to think that if I had enough free time and income to play golf every day, I could spend that time making a big impact out in the world instead. As I had the opportunity to get to know the golfers, I learned that many of them owned businesses. It peeked my curiosity, and at a young age, I was determined to start a business of my own. The only problem was that I was eighteen years old with no mentor, credit, or credibility to start a business. Heck, I showed up to my job interviews with clip-on ties and over-sized suits. It was a far cry from anyone taking me seriously. How was I going to be able to share my passion with others? How in the world was I going to start a business doing it?

My first business was direct sales, and for years, I struggled. Luckily, I had a good coach who told me to invest in personal development. I read books and attended conferences. Although my dreams and visions stretched further, I didn't have any applicable skills that I could use to get results. I felt like I was motivated more than ever — and also broke more than ever. So I went back to my mentors and asked them to tell me what I needed to do to be successful. I assured them that no matter what it was, I would do it. After that, I got my very first experiences making calls out of the yellow pages, searching for potential customers, and pounding the pavement. After doing that for years, I still had no success. Looking back, I was a short kid with a pencil thin mustache and haircut that was quite urban. Recognizing that my presentation could have been a big part of the problem- I was determined to figure out how to be successful!

As a dedicated student of business, I would stay up late at night watching videos on leadership. With little time to spare, I had little time for activities that weren't in alignment with where I wanted to go. My environment wasn't idyllic for a striving entrepreneur either. My friends told me to give it up and play it safe. Even though my mentors directed me in the right direction they informed me that chances were still against me. The reality was that the odds were against me. Regardless of my circumstances, this dream was too engrained in me, and I made a decision that failure would not be an option. I discovered a deep purpose within me that would give me the drive to break through the resistance of a big vision. I had a huge desire to help people, and I knew I had to find a way to make a living doing what I loved. I couldn't give up. I gave it everything I had to learn and apply as much as I could. After four years of hard work and sacrifice, I had nothing to show for it-- I had no friends, no money, and no hope for a future. Believe it or not, I quit! I felt worse than when I started. Sacrificing my youth with no hope for a future… I became bitter, and I lost belief in myself-- I was flat out depressed.

My perspective about business changed when I began to study marketing online. I was dabbling with Internet marketing concepts and was intrigued by the concept of growing a business on the Internet. A friend of mine was having a lot of success selling wellness products through a membership program. When I got a call to meet with him I was very apprehensive to look at any more business ideas. I tried to resist getting involved, but it was hard to hold onto my ego and pride especially since I didn't have any reason to be proud at that time in my life—So I took a chance and went for it!

Finally, I began making some income. I used the extra income to invest in social media coaches, and studied the inns and outs of Internet marketing by attending seminars regularly. My income kept on growing, and I learned valuable information from some of the most influential people online. I invested tens of thousands of dollars to learn the best practices in Internet marketing-- It finally came together! Combining the best principles of leadership, and the best principles of Internet marketing-- my business exploded making more than a million dollars in sales! I built my first community online and for the first time, business felt easy. I was able to do what I loved, experience things I couldn't imagine, and not to mention the fulfillment I was able to experience from the difference I was making. I realized the power of social media, and my only regret was that I wish I had mastered it sooner than I did.

Here is where my life turned once again-- I had a famous "aha!" moment. The thought came to me: *"I built an audience who knows me and trusts me. If I can have success selling someone else's products, why don't I create and sell my own? I could make a bigger impact and reach more people."* So that's what I did. I quickly began to replace my income. It was then that I realized the power of having a social network.

I began to understand that if you position yourself right, and package your brand and message, then with the right marketing strategies, you can make a killing doing whatever it is you love. So I encourage you to follow the strategies I share in this book because the benefits and rewards can last you a lifetime.

STRATEGY ONE

Leaders Are Great at Positioning

"If you don't become an expert at what you do, someone else will."

— Adam Flores

Have you ever wondered what makes some brands higher in demand than others? I began to study market trends due to the lack of demand from my own service and products. So here I was, ready to go out into the world and make a serious impact, to find that I had no clue as to how to spread my message! Meanwhile, many associates I've known for years had great businesses generating great income. I was committed to figuring out how someone could work less than I did, and still generate more business on a consistent basis. Not to mention, this associate charged more for the exact same service—I wanted to know the secret formula. I wanted to position myself so that "my" brand and story could generate that kind of income and make it work for me. So I asked myself, "What is the one activity that I can do again and again consistently that will position me to be the expert in what I do to attract customers into my business?" It was a simple question, and the answer was to invest in my positioning.

What is Positioning?

Positioning is everything that increases your social credibility and solidifies your expertise on a subject, so when the time comes to promote a product or service, you have the best chance to be selected by the consumer. It's the one thing that successful leaders spend a lot of time investing in. Good positioning will sell for you, set you up to attract customers, and create a following that are already interested in what you are doing.

Although sales were on the rise, I wasn't positioned to generate traffic to my social sites. For a long while, I was stuck in the routine of doing activities that produced results, not activities that would allow me to be a great influence online. I knew a great place to start was to create videos and tools that would illustrate my ability to serve my audience. I had to paint a clear picture of my story and share it in a compelling way—one that defined my level of expertise. This step was absolutely crucial for potential clients interested in my products and services to know with confidence that they have struck gold!

A defining moment in my business came when I made a phone call to a prospect on my lead list. This prospect had been following my content, videos, website, and even watched a few testimonials on my site. When I was finally able to contact him by phone, he was overly excited and a bit anxious to talk to me—seemly star struck! I was taken back by the notion that a complete stranger would consider me to have that much clout. It was a defining moment, as it was the first time I didn't have to prove myself. My site material influenced the prospect—and all I had to do was tell him how the program worked in order for him to sign up to get started. I call that the "wow factor"! When your content can "wow" your prospects before ever connecting with them personally, you have definitely established great positioning.

Many years of hard work is what it took to develop my image, build the social proof, and credibility necessary to be highly respected by those following me. It's something I continue to work on… Having clout is extremely rewarding in order to have a higher level of influence on others without actually being there in person. My social sites, social proof, and websites—do it all for me. When it comes time for me to launch a new product, start developing a fresh idea, or get others involved in a program, it's easier knowing I already have their trust.

So where do you begin to invest in your positioning so you can have leverage in the business, organization, or program you are involved in? I believe it starts with getting clarity on your **message**. What message do you want to articulate to your audience?

A good message should reveal the big picture problem you are aiming to solve. In order to get an audience to back you, they need to know what you stand for. A good message is consistent and congruent throughout the content of the brand. The message should position you to attract your ideal audience. If you are not clear on what your message is, I put together a simple three-question framework that will help you identify your message.

Take a moment to answer the question below.

- **What result do I desire for my audience?**

- **What is the problem that is stopping my audience from getting the result they want?**

- **How can I relate to their struggles and what has to change in order for them to get out of their situation?**

- **How can I help them get the result they desire?**

A great message connects to the aspirations and struggles of your audience. If you can identify what your audience wants, why they are not getting it, and how you can lead them to the solution, they will be compelled to understand how you can lead them to the result. Keep in mind the power in your message is in your ability to relate to the pains and problems your audience are going through and how you can lead them out.

Through consistent messaging, your audience will gain clarity on how you can help them.

What is Your Bold Promise?

Sometimes the humility within us can cause us to be reserved when sharing how we can help others get results. We often don't want to be perceived by others as someone who is bragging about our accomplishments. At the same time, we can't stay quite about our ability to help others. We need to be able to affectively communicate the results we can provide for others so they will have clarity on how we can help them. We do this through a **bold promise.**

A **bold promise** is a statement of the specific value that you or your organization can provide for others. Your bold promise is especially attractive when you can add a time frame in which you can deliver that particular result.

For example, a successful fitness product came out called *Thin Thighs in 30 Days!* It was a highly successful fitness product. What if the program was called, *"Learn How to Get a Good Body"*? Isn't *Thin Thighs in 30 Days* a more attractive promise? That is why you want to share a clear bold result you can provide for your clients. If you are hesitant to do so, I'm giving you permission right now to share your promise with the world so others will know how you can help them. Don't be afraid to claim your expertise and share your bold promise with others. If you are reading this book, you know you have something great to offer the world and I want you to feel free to share it. Don't hold back any longer because other people need you.

"Well Adam, not everyone will get the same result. How can I promote a promise that I can't guarantee?" If this is your reservation, I get it. However, your job is to show others what is possible from the results you have had personally, or the results you have helped clients get in the past. You can't control the result of everyone due to the fact that everyone is different. Don't feel obligated to make sure everyone gets results. Does the gym owner feel guilty when the majority of the members don't show up after a few weeks? Instead, the gym owner focuses on making sure the members who do go regularly are having a good experience. Your job is to share what you know and believe to be true. Share what is possible and at the worst-case scenario, you may provide something that may be a critical step in their journey toward their goals or objectives.

Everything you say in your messaging and in your bold promise should lead toward one direction—and this is to solve a problem for your audience. Think about "how" you want others to perceive you. If you were going to be known as a professional in one area what would it be? The content you create, sites you build, and social platforms should work to paint a picture of your experience for your audience. They should align and validate your expertise on a particular subject. When it comes time for you to ask your audience to follow your cause or buy from you, your audience shouldn't have to question what you do or how you can help them.

I remember one time I was in a hot tub with some friends at a resort, and this older man eased his way in. He introduced himself and said, "Hi my name is Glenn Willis, and I am the best there is at what I do." Everyone in the hot tub couldn't help but ask, "What exactly do you do?" He replied, "I'm the best handy man in the south bay. I haven't had to look for business since I started introducing myself this way thirty years ago. People remember me as being the best there is at what I do. Even when I get a referral, my clients tell their friends that I'm the best handy man in the South Bay. Next time their friends need any home repairs, they always think about me."

To this day, my friends and I talk about Glenn. It was such a genius introduction because everyone remembers him for that. I wonder how many other handy men could change their businesses if they took this approach? For now, they are missing out while Glenn Willis is establishing himself as the authority. This concept is no different on social media. Your promise should peak curiosity with your audience.

Your promise should also incorporate what you do for a living. If you're a nutritionist for example, you could share what you do with your audience by saying, "I help people double their energy with my special 90 day meal plan". Most amateur experts do not have a promise and would simply introduce themselves solely as a nutritionist. Having a consistent title with a promise will highlight the result you can provide and make people remember you for what you do. (Make sure your promise reveals your specialty in a specific niche while appealing to the majority. You don't want to have a promise too specific that it's unrelatable to the majority of your audience.)

Once you identify your promise, it will help you anywhere you go. A really good promise will spark the curiosity of your target audience. If you can get them to ask, "How do you do that?" then you will have more opportunities to articulate what you do in a way that may open the door for you to acquire a new buyer or someone who may inbox you requesting for more information.

If you have any trouble deciding what you want to be known for, then you can think about the problems that face your audience every day. Usually there is a pain that you can alleviate or a problem you can solve for them. The pain may be physical or mental, or maybe they need a skill-set in order to reach their goals in a particular area. Regardless of whether you offer a product or a service, ask yourself how can you solve a problem for your audience, and then use your title to define how you can help them.

Take a moment and answer these three powerful questions:

- **"What exactly do I want to be known for?"**

- **"What clear results can I provide for others?"**

- **"What is my bold promise?"**

What if I don't have Results Yet? Can I Still Have Success?

One of the most common concerns among my students is their lack of credibility. They often fear they are not good enough because they don't have results to promote or highlight to their audience. Sometimes they feel other people won't listen because they aren't credible yet. The reality is, that credibility can be established many different ways, and it doesn't always established through your results.

One way you can establish credibility is by interviewing people who are the highest authority in your field of work. It's a way you can borrow the credibility of someone else with more success than yourself. You can be viewed as having credibility because you are associated with them. By doing so, you are also adding value in the eyes of your audience by bringing someone of a higher expertise who can deliver value. Your audience will appreciate you for this added value and hold you in a higher esteem due to your ability to connect with higher associations.

The other way you can establish credibility is to become a researcher in your field of work. If you have invested a lot of time or money to learn a specific topic, you can leverage certifications, specific knowledge, and claim a level of expertise by doing your due diligence in your topic of study.

Find a method you feel comfortable with. Leverage it to gain authority in your topic. Then others will be more likely to choose you when it comes time for them to make a buying decision.

Be the Boss and Be the Best

Over the years, as I've studied social consumer behavior—I've discovered a few tried and tested truths. One of those truths is that people want to follow the ultimate authority on a given subject. When you are positioned as the best, people assume you must have the best information or product that will give them their desired results. In their minds, they have the best chance at reaching their desired outcome through your product or service. This phenomenon happens when the buyer often feels privileged; they have peace of mind knowing they just got access to the best product, service, or information. When this phenomenon occurs, they are often willing to pay top dollar for it. When you have this type of positioning, you now have one of the most powerful forces at work for you, and this is called **authority**. When you have authority you have one of the highest levels of influence — and influence is one of the greatest assets on social media. If you have influence, then people happily follow you, talk about you, share your content, buy from you, and tell everyone else to buy from you.

If you commit to becoming an authority, it's one of the greatest leverages you can have working for you. With everyone searching for information online through social sites or search engines, it helps to have a reputation for being one of the best at what you do. Here's the reality: Most people who appear to be the best online aren't always the best! I'm sure you have come across people who seem less knowledgeable in a particular area than you, yet somehow; they are the one who everyone follows. So the question is, what makes them the authority? The answer is better positioning.

To become an authority, you have to be willing to let yourself value what you know in the highest esteem. This is the single most difficult thing to accept, because nobody wants to think of themselves as the best at what they do. Most people would rather question if their knowledge or results are valid. Many of my students have told me, "Adam, I'm not good enough. I don't know enough." I follow up by asking them, "When will you ever be good enough? When will you ever know enough?" At the end of the day, isn't it a matter of perspective? What if I were to ask you right now, "Do you know more about the subject you study or the field in which you work than most people do?" Do you trust in your ability to find the answers if you don't know something? Can you help people with what you already know? How can you highlight what you know in a way that encourages others to learn from you or buy from you versus everyone else out there?

I believe you have the answers to what people are looking for, and your experiences and your story make you unique and valuable to the market place. It's so easy to question yourself and wonder if you really have what it takes to be the authority in what you do. Who are you *not* to be the authority? I want to empower you to claim your expertise and become the "go to" person in whatever you do. If you don't become an expert at what you do, someone else will. I'd rather it be you. We are in a connected world with billions of people, and there is enough room for all of us to attract our fair share of the market. It doesn't take getting the masses to follow you in order for you to make a difference and a fortune. Get to the place of peace within yourself and give yourself permission to let your light shine.

Take a Moment

- **"What am I doing to position myself to be the best at what I do?"**

- "What actions can I take to become an authority in what I do?"

In a moment, I'm going to share ten of the most proven strategies to become the authority at what you do. I will also share the psychology behind why these methods work. It's very important to me that you understand these strategies are not, in any form, a way to manipulate people, but instead a way to help position you to serve people on a greater level. You now can appreciate that understanding people is the key to being effective on social media. In a broken world full of false hope, people want to find answers, and it's often the good, genuine people who get left behind in their search. Understand that hitting your stride will take time. However, if you apply these strategies with the highest of ethics, your level of influence on social media will skyrocket.

Here are ten proven strategies on how to become the authority at what you do:

1. Write a Book on the Topic in which You Claim Your Expertise

Writing a good book is so easy these days and it's one of the single most important ways to become credible on a subject. As people learn from the value in your book, they look up to you as the teacher. It opens their mind to learning from you, because you appear to have more knowledge on the subject. If that's not the case, well then shame on them for not writing a book on what they know.

I remember procrastinating on writing my first book for so many years because I questioned my credibility as a young entrepreneur. I thought, *"There are so many people who are older than I am, write better than I do, and even people who have more important things to say."* Until one day, I saw one of my friends who had written a book, and had several doors open for him that weren't available before. I saw the way people responded to him, and I watched his level of influence go through the roof. That's when I thought, *"If he can do it... I know I can do it!"*

I started out by writing a small eBook. As I began to call myself a self-published author, people started to treat me differently, and the people in my social networks started to take me seriously. It was at that point that I was able to charge more for my coaching. This even brought in more students because they wanted to learn how to apply the principles I shared in the book.

Writing a book allowed me to also leverage my ideas with more people. The ideas I had were valuable, and I knew that people could benefit from them. After publishing my ideas in a small eBook, people would message me in the middle of the night, letting me know how much they enjoyed reading it—This added so much meaning to my life, and for those who wanted to continue their journey with me as students... the eBook allowed me to serve them in that way.

Writing a book also opens doors to connect with people of higher influence. Leaders love to connect with authors. It's a bridge that will allow you to get in the door with other influential people who can promote you and endorse you.

The more you can share those partnerships on social media, the more clout you have, as well as credibility. Hopefully as you have read this text, you have also seen by now that writing a book is extremely helpful in contributing to your positioning.

I believe what stops people from publishing a book is that they don't think they have the credentials, the fancy "PhD" title after their last name, or that they haven't become successful yet. I do know from experience, that you don't have to have monumental results to write a book—You can borrow the ideas of other people you have studied. If you have results of your own, that's great! As long as you don't make claims that aren't true or misleading, then by all means, what are you waiting for? If you are a horrible writer, the solution is to find people online who will edit your work at a reasonable cost. If you are worried about not getting picked up by a publisher, don't worry about it—You can always self-publish.

I spend so much time in this area because the foundation of success through social media comes from positioning and leveraging your credibility to attract a following. Writing a book can make you an authority in whatever you write about, and it will cause more people to trust you. In the last chapter I have emphasized why this is a key element to understanding what gets people to buy from you. If you haven't gotten around to it yet, write a book!

2. Teach Your Audience through Valuable Content

One of the biggest shifts in my business happened when I stopped seeing my potential customers as prospects, and instead saw them as my students. Not only does this perspective cause you to take on more of a leadership role with your following online, it subconsciously makes you the teacher to your potential students. Nobody likes a sales person, but everybody loves a good teacher. When you become someone who *teaches* people, their perception of who you are begins to change in their mind, your social credibility increases, and if the content you post is done correctly… it will also motivate your followers to continue to learn more about what you do and how you do it.

Making videos is a great way to build your positioning and become an authority in what you do, especially when you have dozens of videos on a topic.

When your videos exceed the expectations of the viewer, and you consistently make them over a period of time—you will get positive feedback and referrals! When others validate that your content is good, it creates a positive social proof. I remember when my first video reached fifty shares, I was ecstatic! If each person had five hundred friends, that video could have potentially reached twenty-five thousand people.

I took this source of authority for granted when I first started this venture, because I felt that making videos was a waste of time. The reason was due to my disappointment that my first videos only had a few likes, and I didn't see how they could bring in revenue… so I stopped making them. The funny thing is, when I stopped making the videos, people began to make inquiries as to when I was going to upload more videos— It was then that I realized if you make videos, people will actually watch them…even if they don't click "Like". A high percentage of my customers are drawn through my videos where they can get onto my subscriber list and stay updated on any upcoming events or products I have available.

Posting videos is vital to your business and serves as an opportunity to share your gifts, ideas, and visions with the world. You'll never know how the concepts that are shared can impact someone's life. There have been several videos that have helped me along my journey, even though I did not always become a customer or client of each person. Don't take for granted the lives you can touch by sharing your thoughts, ideas, and wisdom with the world, because you never know who is watching and who can benefit from what you have to share.

3. Interview Influential People

One of the easiest ways to gain authority on a topic is to interview people who have a high level of experience or results in your field. -You are not only bringing value to yourself, but to your audience through the experiences and knowledge of others. Sometimes the expert you have created great rapport with may even share your interview on their page, and this is how you can become credible through association. Interviewing is a great way to establish partnerships and serve your audience. All you need to accomplish your mission is a live stream, or video camera, and you are good to go!

4. Share Client Results and Case Studies

If you have specific people who you have helped with your product or service, you can share their results and responses through blogs, photos, live testimonials, or videos. You can share responses before and after, so your audience can see the specific results you helped them attain.

This is a great way to get your potential customers to see that you are a professional at what you do. The more stories and examples you can share of the transformation of your clients or students, the more prospective followers will place their faith in you as a professional.

You often see this strategy displayed in the weight loss and anti-aging industries. This technique can be used in any industry where results are measurable. Even in the beginning, if you give your service away for free in exchange for a testimonial,–it's worth it. If you have positive results with your clients, share them. Your primary goal is to increase your influence as soon as possible. People will not always believe it when they see it, although, if they continue to see the results it's only a matter of time before they begin to wonder how you can help them.

5. **Run Campaigns to Build Your Following**

When people notice that you have a large number of likes and followers, they tend to automatically assume you are important. Many people think it's a popularity contest and believe you have to be a celebrity to have such a large following. In actuality, you just need to run ads or collaborate with other influential people in order to get a new audience to like your page.

Sometimes to gain influence immediately, businesses or individuals will run ads to build a following quickly and build social proof on their profile. That way, when a new potential customer visits the social page, they see thousands of likes already and assume it's a highly credible page. Although this route can cost some money and time up front, it's a great way to build social proof quickly.

6. Emphasize Your Experience

Often times people tend to undermine their experiences. Do not undervalue your observations and findings that can save your prospects a lot of time and money. We are in a world that wants answers fast. If you can use what you have learned through your experiences to help people short-cut the process and find the information they are looking for, people will respect the time you have invested in the development of your skills. When you can utilize your number of years of experience in a particular field, it serves as a major credibility piece, and it's human nature to want to learn from those who have more experience than we have.

If you make a video, perform an interview, or write a post— you emphasize the time you have invested. Time invested is something others can't short-cut, so they have to respect what you have sacrificed to know what you know. Own your expertise.

7. Highlight Your Education and Awards

One of the most culturally accepted forms of credibility are your credentials, which may include a BA, BS, MA, or PhD. You can include your credentials after book titles, ask people who interview you to mention them, add them to the end of your name and to logos as part of your branding.

If you have specific knowledge that you have learned outside of a university, it tends to also carry a high level of value, because it usually a niche of knowledge that most people aren't willing to go out and pay for or invest time to discover. Most people don't want to spend money to learn from a specialist or a coach, but they want the information you have learned from those people. You can leverage the time and money you have invested in coaches and experts by asking other people to invest in you in order to access your information and knowledge.

If you have any seminars that you have paid for, or conferences you have attended, definitely highlight those as your continuing education. People like to learn from someone who specializes in an area. When you become a specialist, it's human nature for people to hold you in high regard in that area of expertise.

Awards can also be leveraged as a credibility piece. If you have specific awards or have been nominated for an exclusive promotion or award, you can highlight those accomplishments or nominations. People love to learn from the best and it is awesome when you can claim your victories.

Now I want to be clear, these accolades or credentials are supposed to be used to persuade people, not just brag about. As leaders, you want to show others that you are an authority so they are comfortable and confident learning from you or in some cases partnering with you. If you can articulate you expertise through your social media sites, people are highly receptive when they have the opportunity to learn from the best.

8. Partner with Celebrities

When you get the opportunity to associate with a celebrity, people often assume you are at a social status that is above the norm. It gives you a perceived value because you are drafting off of the credibility of someone else. Although you may not actually have a personal relationship with a celebrity, there are still ways that you can leverage their social status. For example, you can take a picture of them holding your book, have them write something nice about you that you can promote to your audience, interview them, or take pictures with them at the event you attend.

People think that celebrities are often out of reach, when in fact they are highly accessible if you have a reason to approach them. Celebrities love to connect with people who have a good cause, who have a vision that can help others, and who offer to help others.

I remember being in the hallway of a resort when I met a highly successful entrepreneur. She is one of the most successful women in the country in the business world. After a short chat, I told her that she inspired me, and I was wondering if there was any way I could help her with anything. She was really surprised that I came to her with such an open heart and willingness to serve. It was a very gratifying conversation. That being said, if you can approach celebrities the right way, they are great assets and serve as social proof, creating a perceived value by your audience.

9. Build a High Quality Brand

If you have a page that looks run down, with cheap photography or videography, or if you are displaying images of yourself in unprofessional places or situations, people may not take you seriously as a professional. If you can invest in building a high-quality brand, it's more aesthetically pleasing, your brand image will carry more value, and on occasion you can charge more for the value of your product or service. Think about the people you follow online? Do they have high-resolution and high-quality design? Building a high quality brand will add value to positioning yourself as an authority.

10. Have Your Clients Promote You through Testimonials

People often believe something is good when someone else tells them it's good. If there is a client that you have provided value for, ask them to write a testimonial or give you a shout out on their next live stream. It's one of the highest honors when someone values their experience with you so much that they promote you to their own audience.

Not only will you attract more followers, you will attract more business if that person has a circle of influence that is like-minded. It's a great first impression and automatically gives you a certain level of credibility and clout. Next time you give great service to someone, ask him or her to share their experience on their social site. It is a great way to have others promote you as the authority.

Embrace the Challenge

Some people don't think about using social media as a platform to show credibility, and they just use it to post random life events. If you shift your mentality to use it as a platform to share your gifts and display your credibility, when you run promotions (which I'm going to teach you how to do), your audience is going to love to hear what you have to say. It's your job as leaders to stand out above the rest so that your audience is open-minded and learns from you. If you can do a great job of displaying your authority, then you often have the ability to influence your audience to make a certain buying decision, to follow your causes, or to purchase your services.

I know that sometimes it can feel overwhelming to keep up and stay relevant on social media. My encouragement to you is to not compare yourself to others. Run your own race. My goal is encourage you to invest in your positioning so your story and image can speak for you. If you want to apply these strategies simultaneously at a high level, then you can, or you can use the strategies as you go through life. Sometimes it's overwhelming trying to rise above the noise when life has worries of its own. Instead of seeing effective positioning as more work, see it as a challenge. Practice using these strategies one at a time and let your profile come together into one great testament of your leadership. The reality is that you don't have to be the absolute best in order to get a following online. You just want to be the best to your audience, and that is usually good enough. I believe you are amazing and talented, and I want the world to see you shine. You might be the exact person who other people are waiting for before they decide to jump in for themselves.

STRATEGY TWO

The Leadership Package

*"Most people aim to create a brand.
Leaders aim to create an experience."*

—Adam Flores

Imagine walking into a café with an earthy ambiance. There is a nice urban jazzy flow of music. You can hear the milk steaming and you can't help but take in the aroma. It's now time for your morning cup of coffee. You take your coffee and pour in a bit of cream and sugar, stir it around, and sip it a few times until it's just right.

What makes this experience special when you could have purchased coffee at the market for half the price? What caused you to spend twice as much for the exact same product? What makes the coffee you purchased valuable at the price you paid for it? There are many different reasons that I'm sure come to your mind. If we were to sum them up, it would come down to one thing—your experience!

What makes an experience? The setup of the coffee shop, the people, the music, the brand, the product, and how that brand and product make you feel. All of those factors play a role in creating an experience. This experience causes you to go out of your way and pay more, and at the end of the day you don't think twice about the money you have spent. If people were attracted to buying the product and saving money, grocery stores would be packed with coffee consumers. However, that is not the case. We are a culture that seeks after brands that make us feel a certain way.

For that reason, how you package your look, your story, and social experience for your audience will determine how others perceive and feel about you. Unfortunately, the culture we live in makes decisions about who we are and what we represent. People make these decisions instantaneously, and they are slow to change their mind. So you have to package your message, ideas, and concepts in a way that create an experience for your audience.

In this chapter, I aim to focus on three main ideas that will help you create a highly influential brand package:

- How to create the "WOW" factor for your audience

- How to create a "Customer Journey" for your followers

- How to leverage your brand to connect with your "Target Audience"!

If you can master these three elements, you can increase your following, your influence, your conversion from followers to buyers, and the price people are willing to pay for what you have to offer. There is an opportunity to control some level of perception that your audience has of you. If you can influence their perception, it's only a matter of time before their perception becomes a reality. The social world can only know you based on what you project yourself to be. This can also be dangerous if you portray yourself to be something you are not. Make sure to use this principle ethically and with honesty. We want to package your brand in a way they will be able to see you are a pro at what you do. Your brand is powerful and should always operate in full integrity.

Create the "Wow Factor" in Your Brand

The "wow" factor is all about "wowing" the viewer with the visual aesthetics of your page. There is an invisible influence that occurs when the feel of your brand is aesthetically pleasing. Your photography, videography, color combination, design, and value that you offer on your page, all contribute to an experience. When your brand is packaged correctly, it sends an immediate message to the viewer that you are a professional at what you do.

Unfortunately, many people don't invest in their image because it's not a cheap process and they don't see the potential for return on their investment. Instead, many entrepreneurs will focus on driving traffic, growing a following, getting good engagement on their posts, and lead generation. The reality is that you can still make a lucrative income online without a brand; however, long term you are limiting your success. There is no question that building a quality brand will increase your social influence and impact. This ultimately will lead into a greater increase in client conversions. In addition, good branding will do the majority of selling for you.

I remember a particular instance when someone messaged me for my services, and she happened to be a graduate from a prestigious University in California. When we got on the phone she said, "Adam! Oh my God it's you! I can't believe I'm actually on the phone with you. I just want to let you know that I have watched all of your videos, watched your testimonials, and I'm so looking forward to working with you. All I need to know is how much it will cost and I'm ready to get started."

Inside I was bursting with excitement in complete awe of what I was hearing. While she was talking to me I was a little distracted in my own thoughts. I said to myself, "Finally, someone who values what I have to offer and I don't have to convince her. This is a miracle." Previously, I had to always convince others of the value I could bring to them. It would get exhausting having to explain myself to others over and over again. This time, my brand did the selling and convincing for me. It was the easiest sale I had ever made and it felt amazing! That was the first time I realized the power of having a brand.

I know at times putting a strong emphasis on image can feel like a shallow subject. The reality is that investing in your brand is really about positioning yourself to help more people. In order for people to follow your vision or follow you in business, they need to feel comfortable. We are in a world that needs to see some level of social proof. We no longer automatically take people at their word for the services they offer without doing our due diligence. If you don't have the tools and the image to support your claims, the customer will find someone else who does. If you really want to help people, then build your brand in a way to attract the people that need your services.

Building Your Brand

When it comes to building your actual personal brand, I recommend finding the absolute best designers and team to create it for you. I remember for years I tried to do it the inexpensive way and outsource it to designers overseas to save money. My brand never stayed consistent, and I ended up having to go back and forth for months with revision after revision. It was a very costly experience and that is why it's better to invest more upfront and have it done correctly. If not, you may be loosing many potential customers that have gone to someone else due to better branding—Don't let them take your customers. Let's make YOU the 'go-to' person for their needs!

Years ago, I realized that many of my students were struggling with building their brand correctly. They struggled with messaging, design work, brand consistency, and especially videography. So I decided to put together the *Dream Factory—* a program inside of our *Business Club Academy.* The *Dream Factory* is our studio where clients can come in and have their brand built from scratch. It consist of world-class videography, photography, web development, and you even get access to a brand manager that helps you identify your message. It's a great way to get everything done in one place—not to mention you save a great amount of time.

If you can get access to a program like, the *Dream Factory*, it really makes things simple and effective. You can get your brand up and running in a short amount of time so you can focus on income producing activities that are going to grow your business. As a business owner or a leader of an organization, you should not be learning how to build a website. You should be delegating the task to someone else so you can stay focused on what you are good at.

For this reason, I don't recommend hiring a family member or friend who has been developing sites as a hobby. They have their own bias views as to how 'your' site should look, and this can create havoc due to the personal nature of your relationship with them—not to mention, the lack of objectivity that can damage the image you're trying to brand. Trust me I've seen it happen. The Dream Factory ensures that you get affordable, high-quality professional assistance through our intranet in order to customize YOUR dream! So many people get caught in thinking it's more complicated than it is. People who are not tech-savvy tend to avoid new ways of doing things because it seems overwhelming... However, things are made so simple now. The image of your brand is something you don't want to leave in the hands of an amateur. Businesses across the board are getting more modern by the day—you don't want your business looking outdated by attempting to do it yourself. You want the best, and you shouldn't settle for less. Technology is nothing to be afraid of these days. If it is still holding you back, it's because you haven't taken the time to see what resources are available today.

Let's create an experience for your potential customers that when they see your brand—it's a true reflection of your business, and who you are as an individual. Your brand will speak to your audience often before you do. Think about how your style makes people feel. You want everything to be color-coordinated, and have a level of cleanliness and simplicity to make a pleasant experience for the viewer when they come to visit your site. A simple way to choose the style that best fits your brand is to study other people in your field of work and pick and choose what you like best. Look at their style, colors, and the feel of the page. Take what you like from other sites and apply it to your own. If you are guilty of having a style or an image you know isn't the feel you should have for your business, just have it modified—This is an area worth investing in.

Take a Moment

- **Does Your Brand Image Create the "wow" experience?**

- **Is there any area that you need to re-brand? If so, what adjustments do you plan on making after reading this section?**

Creating Your Customer Journey

I remember after I completed my brand for the first time, a prospect from across the country messaged me on one of my social pages. Long story short, he told me I had inspired him greatly and that one-day he hoped to meet me. Out of curiosity I asked him, "How did you find me?" He went on to say that a video that I posted intrigued him, which then led him to click on the link to my website. There, he watched a video on my story, looked at my videos, and watched testimonials. He subscribed to my email list. After getting a few of my emails, he reached out to me to help him in his business. When he explained the journey he went through, I was ecstatic because it was exactly how I envisioned the process when I built my brand. I call this process the customer journey! It's the process that leads your following into becoming clients.

What does your customer journey look like? How are you leading your followers through a strategic process so they can become your client? As you layout the customer journey, here are some of the elements that you should include along the process:

1. **Your Story**

I believe the most powerful part of the customer journey is your story. Don't we all have a story to tell? I believe your story is one of the best marketing tools you can have, yet so many people never share it—why do you think that is? People are moved when you share your passion for what you do and why you do it. In my coaching programs, I coach my students on how to package their story in a way that is compelling and intriguing. If you can learn to tell your story through social media, this story can also work for you by generating income while you are sleeping. You never know who is watching it from around the world. If you package your story correctly, you never know who will be moved by it and want what you have—a great business!

2. **Testimonials**

Think about all of the people you have helped get results. Often, we forget to include testimonials of lives that we have impacted through our businesses or organizations. I had a client who had impacted so many people through her consulting business. When I went to her site, there was no evidence of the impact she has made. Unfortunately, this happens more often than not. We forget to share the stories of the clients we have helped. Testimonials serve as a great way to communicate the value that you can bring to others.

3. Free Value

With so many free offers you see online you can't just give away anything for free and expect to get your client to subscribe. You need to provide a real solution that will help them get a real result. If you can get them from point A to B, there is a good chance they will seek out your services to get C and D. You can do this by offering a free video series, free access to a private social group, free access to a webinar, free access to a guide, etc. The goal is to continue the journey by having them subscribe so you can continue to develop the relationship on the backend of your brand.

4. Campaign

Congrats! If you have got them to become a subscriber it's time to lead them toward becoming a client! Once they become a subscriber they now should get a series of valuable content that will show them how you are going to help them get the result they are looking for. You can do this through videos, blogging, or inviting them to live webinar where you can educate them more specifically on how you can help them get results.

5. The Call-to-Action

After dripping educational and "trust building" content it's now time for the call-to-action. This is the time to give them clear directions on how to become a client. This can be a free strategy call, an invite for a free tour of your facility, a checkout page where they can order your product directly, or an invite to fill out an application to your program. Make sure to create urgency with deadlines and incentives for taking action. If they don't become a client, send out another campaign adding more value and then lead them into another call-to-action.

With all of the pieces involved in creating an amazing experience for your followers it can feel overwhelming at times if you don't have any of the elements in place already. The good news is that once you have the path laid out, then you can focus on driving traffic into your funnels and allow the process to work for you. Figure out what you need to build and work on putting the pieces of the puzzle together one step at a time.

Target Audience

Now it's time for the big question I get asked often, "Adam, how do I find my target audience to market to?" I think so many people get caught up in relating to a specific demographic and they often fear being too broad with their marketing approach. The reason is that for many years marketers have taught that you must find a specific demographic before you start marketing. This frame of thinking was intended toward marketing niche products. For example, if you were to market an expensive vacuum cleaner or a luxury retail item, you would need to know the target audience in order to be affective with your marketing efforts.

However, in today's time we are marketing information and content. It is no longer about identifying a narrow and specific target audience before marketing to them. Instead, what you're looking for are specific targeted interests. The new wave of marketing is about appealing to the aspirations and interests of your audience, and allowing your target audience to reveal itself as they respond to your content. For example, I have students that are different in age, social economic status, and ethnic background. If you were to attend one of my live events, you would realize that I don't have a target demographic other than the broad category of entrepreneurs. The reason why is because I market to the aspirations and interests of my audience therefore, I attract people of all backgrounds.

Say for instance, you had a fitness business and you wanted to target women between 27-40 who are overweight. Why set your mind on that demographic? If you market to struggles and aspirations of losing weight and make that your focus, you may attract the 22 year old that is looking to get into shape. My advice in this area is to make a list of struggles and aspirations that your audience will relate to. Your target audience will reveal itself as your promote your content.

Also, don't be hesitant to experiment with different styles of delivering your content in order to see what you audience likes best. What I love about social media is that it allows you to creatively promote what you do in different ways. Not everyone is moved the same way. Some people are attracted to entertainment, others are attracted to education, and others love things that inspire them. In regards to packaging, it's all about delivering your message to your potential audience in a way they want to see it. If you can learn to do that, your engagement, shares, and activity will be much higher.

Find out how you can creatively share things that will captivate the attention of your audience. Sometimes it's simply taking a step back and thinking about what would make a unique video or post that can still convey the message to your followers. If you continue to add unique posts over a period of time, then your profile will be distinguishable from everyone else's in the social space. Sometimes it can be outside of your comfort zone to do something different. If you don't, how will you ever know what's your capable of?

Make sure that in the process of experimenting you don't dive into the trap of loud interrupting promotions that come off to be extremely "salesy". Unfortunately, many people teach this form of interruption marketing where you flash big red arrows at your links in order to get someone to click on your post. As leaders it's about connecting with your audience. Imagine walking into a store and seeing guys jump out at you wearing red costumes and waving red arrows, trying to get you to buy the items on sale? At first it would probably make you laugh, then after seeing it a thousand times, you would probably be annoyed. Just because something can grab someone's attention doesn't always mean it's a good marketing strategy. Many marketers create posts that jump out at you, but those posts eventually turn the viewer off because they didn't log in to receive that type of engagement.

If you want to relate to your audience and be relevant on the platform you are using, you have to understand what people are looking for so you can optimize your connection with them when you post. Below, I share three key reasons why people log in. Hopefully this will provide a different perspective so you can better understand your viewers.

1. People Desire to Be a Part of a Community and Feel Connected

Most people don't want to be alone. Logging in to social media gives people a sense of connection and belonging. It makes people feel relevant and "in the loop." It's a way to remain connected even when you are not physically together. People are curious by nature, and often don't want to miss something that is going on within their circle of friends and family. Social media fulfills that desire to engage with others regardless of where someone might be in the world.

2. People Want to Be Heard

Most people have ideas or thoughts they wish to share with others in the hopes of being heard. People want others to feel and experience the things that may be on their mind, the places they have been, and the ideas they feel are important. It's human nature for people to want to feel important and be noticed. It's a sense of validation when others like the experiences and thoughts that we share.

3. People Need the Chance to Succeed

Participating in social media is a way to quickly share information about your latest endeavors. People wish to express their creative efforts in the hopes of gaining a following of like-minded people and finding success.

Knowing that these three elements shape the culture of social media, how do your posts stay relevant to other people? In other words, if you want to promote something about your business or organization, how can you promote it in a way that seems natural to your audience? Do you see why aggressive marketing tactics aren't as effective online as much as people think?

If you want to post something with the intent of generating a potential customer, post something that appears natural. For example, you can share a story of a "before and after" experience with a customer you may have had. Post things that reveal human characteristics that people relate to. If people stumble across your post, you want to intrigue them by expressing something that will captivate them. Graphics of your brand do not captivate people, pictures of your products do not captivate people, and discounts off of your product or service don't typically captivate people.

Real experiences, real stories, and real results are what captivate people. I encourage you to look at your posts from the viewer's perspective. Knowing why people log in, would your post captivate them? If not, find a way to express your message differently. It also helps when you determine the social media platform that will be the best use for your style.

Bringing It All Together

Your branding and packaging are not only about your appearance—they are also about your messaging and what you convey to people. You can have the best website, but without delivering compelling and captivating content, people will be less likely to engage with you. Your sites, your design, your content, your style, and your delivery all work together to create an experience. That is what separates leaders from the rest. While most people aim to create a brand, leaders aim to create an experience. Remember the coffee shop at the beginning of the chapter—the experience is what causes people to go out of their way, take action, and pay you more for your service. Packaging is all about creating an experience that will cause people to fall in love with what you do and what you have to offer.

Take a Moment

- **"How can I deliver content in a more creative and entertaining way that will appeal to the struggles or aspirations of my target audience?"**

- **"How can I create a customer journey that will lead them to take action?"**

STRATEGY THREE

Leaders Promote Big

"The best promotions on social media are often the ones that don't look like promotions at all."

— Adam Flores

"Promote your business like you are running for president", I heard once from a good friend. What a great idea I thought to myself. When a nominee runs for president they don't run a promotion, they run a campaign! The campaign doesn't last a day, two days, or three days; it last for over a year! During that process the candidate has a consistent message, he or she addresses the struggles of the country, and boldly claims to provide the solution. Their speech is unwavering, their confidence is bold, and you can feel the passion run through their teeth.

So many people have a burning desire inside to get their message out into the world in a bigger way just as the president does. What stops us from promoting what we do? I could easily list a few things such as fear, uncertainty, lack of confidence, and the list goes on. The truth is that we often don't consider our message to be of great value so we don't promote it out of fear that others won't value it either. You'll never pursue what you don't value.

You may be thinking, "What? That can't be it Adam! Isn't fear stopping me? Don't I have to figure out what limiting thoughts are holding me back?" The answer is no! I'll prove it to you. Image if a guy walked up to you at a cafe and ripped your laptop out of your hands and took off. Would you have to think about the limiting thoughts that are holding you back or would you immediately chase him down to get it back? Of course you would immediately chase him because you value your laptop and value yourself enough to not allow someone to violate you in that way. At that moment, you wouldn't think. Instead, you would spring into action! Why? It is because when you hold something in high value, you'll do anything to get it. It's the same driving force that causes a fireman to run into a burning building—He values another life over his own.

Think about what you value. When it comes time to campaign what opportunity do you value so greatly that nothing can stop you from sharing your message? When you focus on what you truly value, you will feel a fire burning inside of you that will fuel you to get your message out into the world.

Rookies Promote Leaders Campaign

When it comes time to promote our product or service online, it's easy to announce our business or run a quick promotion on an amazing deal we are offering. However, when was the last time you ran a campaign like you were running for president?

If you are reading this book, you have something amazing to offer. Why are you not talking about what you do every single day? I know what you are thinking, "Adam, I don't have time to get on social media everyday and I don't want to come across as salesy". It's only "salesy" if you promote to the same exact audience everyday. The awesome features of online marketing allow you to leverage your message by running ad campaigns to different audiences.

Focus On Your Campaign Objective

When I put a campaign together for a client, the first thing we discover is the objective of the campaign. What exactly are we looking to achieve? For you, that can mean promoting your product or it can be about growing a larger following to bring awareness to your organization or brand. Once you discover your objective think about the struggles and pain points of your audience. For example, if you are promoting a fitness campaign, make sure to address the pain points that your program may have a solution for; such as fatigue, lack of confidence, insecurities, etc. What is stopping them from getting the result that you can provide? (Connecting to the struggles and pain points of your audience will bring connection with them. If all of your focus is on the features, then you will miss the emotional connection of your audience.)

Next, discover your audience by targeting them based off of their interests. Most people make the mistake of assuming their audience. In marketing, you must target and test in order to discover your true audience. You do this through a process called A/B testing.

The goal is to run multiple campaigns to different interests groups. Look at the data to see what interests your audience is responding to the most. Once you identify that, adjust the ads to your campaign and run the ads again to a more targeted audience. Continue this process until you have dialed in your audience interests. (Feel free to connect with our team if you would like advice on this process)

The FEAR of Losing

For so many years I didn't run ads because I was afraid of losing money. I wouldn't see a return right away so I was apprehensive to continue testing my ads. Don't allow fear to stop you. Stay committed until your ad campaign converts into a profit. Then you can focus on scaling your impact.

Outcome of an Ad

Many of my customers ask me which social media platform they should advertise on. I believe it's always best to look at which platform your audience engages with most and start advertising on that one first. Regardless of the platform, there are really only two outcomes you want from running your ads: Either people will become automated customers or they will be customers acquired manually. Let's take a moment and look at the two.

The Manual System

The manual system is a great way to make a lucrative income immediately without having a large list. It requires a personal connection with the potential customer and is more of a hands-on sale. The manual system may include building a relationship with a prospect first or require you to directly interact with a prospect until the sale is made. If you are able message someone directly and pick up the phone to make a sale, you have a higher chance of converting the sale for your product or service.

If you were to run a promotion to acquire a customer manually, your call to action on the ad would be to achieve at least one of the following seven objectives:

1. Have them fill out an opt-in form that includes their phone number so you can make a sale by phone.

2. Have them email you or message you directly, so you can engage in a conversation. This may lead to a phone call or a link you send them where they can purchase your product or service.

3. Direct people into groups where you can live stream to create a community that will be interested in buying your product or service.

4. Invite people to watch a free webinar and call them after the webinar to make a sale.

5. Promote an Interview with an Influencer. After, you can lead them to purchase the product or service.

6. Direct message your target audience. Build a relationship through conversation and make a sale.

7. Run a campaign that will invite them to an event. Make a sale at the event.

The Automated System

Who doesn't want to generate business on autopilot? This is a great way to make sales if you have a huge subscriber list that you don't have time to reach manually. This is one of the reasons why I was attracted to doing business online. It seemed like a dream to have sales come through automation. Since the goal in business is freedom, I wanted to build an automated system so I could spend time doing things I wanted to do. In fact, it wasn't as simple as it looked. It took a lot of my time and money to figure it out.

If you're just starting out, this isn't what I would necessarily recommend as your only marketing plan—unless, you already have a list of people to market to. However, I believe everyone should build an automated system. I remember when I made my first automated sale; I was ecstatic! It's one of the most amazing feelings to sell a product and not physically be there.

Although every marketer wants a business to generate income on autopilot, a cash system to make sales on autopilot, it's important to know the conversions are lower than making sales manually. It takes a large list of subscribers, more traffic, and followers to make automated sales successfully, since there is typically not a personal engagement between you and your audience like you can get with manual marketing.

If you were to run an ad to acquire an automated customer, your call to action on the ad would be to fulfill the following objectives:

1. Lead them to a sales page that sells them a product on the spot. (Typically if you are selling a low-ticket item)

2. Invite them to fill out an opt-in form that leads to an automated email campaign. This may include a few videos that peak curiosity, followed by a sales video that sells for you.

3. Get people to opt-in to watch a free webinar and sell automated on the back-end after they watch the webinar.

4. Sell a low-ticket item with a low-risk buying decision and then automate the upsell to a high-ticket item in the back-end.

5. Ask them to subscribe to your social media channel so you can continue to drip content on them, and then follow up with a "call-to-action" to click on a link that drives them through your sales funnel.

There is a rare exception to these tactics—brand recognition. This approach is usually for larger businesses that sell in stores. Their intention is to get followers and expose their brand to the masses. No call-to-action or opt-in forms required. Often times their products are in stores. They want to continuously promote their brand to you so you are more likely to purchase their product in stores or buy their service when you are ready.

Take a Moment

- **How does your business make sales?**

- **Would you be more interested in setting your business up to acquire customers using automated, manual, or use both systems?**

Promotions MUST Lead to Profits

Although it can be fun when others like and engage with your posts, the priority still needs to be to develop a profit. In order to do so, you must have the right strategies in place. The end result of these strategies is to get the potential buyers to make a buying decision. You want to make sure the posts you promote have an intended purpose of generating profits. It might be an annotated link that pops up after the video that leads them to an opt-in, or maybe it's a call to action to message or email you. The better you can tighten your system, the better you will be able to track your results. When you can track your results, it makes it easier to develop a formula that you can use to generate greater profits.

The Input-Output Formula

From the onset of any promotion campaign, your goal is to identify your input vs. output formula. How much does it cost you to get people into your funnel or sales process, and how much do you make when they become a customer? For example, if you spend $500 per month in ads, how many customers do you need to make a profit?

You need to know the annual value of your customer so you can calculate these numbers. Take into consideration what you make when the customer upgrades to other products or services you may provide throughout the year. Individuals and businesses often undervalue what their customers bring them in revenue, especially when the customers are reoccurring. Once you determine the annual value of your customer, you need to identify how many opt-ins are needed per sale. If you collect phone numbers, than you need to know how many numbers you need per sale. If you connect through messages, you need to know how many messages you need per sale. Once you identify your numbers, you scale up to generate more sales, and you run more promotions to bring in more traffic.

The question I always ask myself is, "If I put in "x" amount of advertising dollars, how many sales do I need to make in order to produce a profit?" If you have never run ads before, you will not know the answer up front. However, If you can determine the number that is required for you to generate a profit, then you can spend more to make more. For example, if you spend $500 a month to generate $2,000 in sales, then $2,000 in ads for the month would make $8,000 in sales. In that case, you would have a 1:4 input-output ratio. If you know your ratio, then it just becomes a numbers game.

It's not uncommon to find people who master the online and social space to find a 1:2 input-output ratio. In those cases, if a person were to spend $10,000 per month in ads, they would make $20,000 for the month in sales. If you have a reverse ratio and you are losing money, then that means you need to adjust your ad until it gets results that are profitable. Sometimes that means tweaking the ad copy, changing the triggers, or using a different tool. After testing different ads, over time you will determine which one is performing the best. If you still can't generate a profit, there is most likely a problem with your positioning, packaging, or sales process. That is why you must always work to improve the different areas of your business.

A Look at the Numbers

Here is an example. Let's say you pay $5,000 to generate 10,000 highly targeted followers. Of the 10,000 highly targeted followers, you continuously promote posts that get 5% to opt-in. In this scenario, your sales funnel is an opt-in form that gathers their name and phone number. That means you would have 500 phone numbers to call at the end of one month(Remember, these are highly targeted leads). Now let's say you call your leads and convert 10% of the 500 numbers. That means you would have made 50 sales. If you had a product that cost the customer $80 per month, then the value of that customer over a year is $960($80 x 12 months). If you multiply 50 sales by the annual value of your customer, you would have made $48,000 for the year. That is only converting 50 people out of 10,000 highly targeted followers that you paid to acquire. That is a .005% conversion rate from followers to customers. Your original investment was $5,000 to acquire the customers. This would have given you a 1:9 input-output ratio, assuming customers stayed the entire year.

The question becomes, "What would happen if you paid $50,000 to generate 100,000 followers?" At a .005% conversion rate from followers to customers, you would have made 500 sales.

500 sales x $960 (annual value of a customer) = $480,000

Note: The input to output ratio is still 1:9

That was an example for making a sale manually. Now let's say you had the sale on automation, meaning you would convert fewer people. If you paid $5,000 to get 10,000 followers and converted 5% to opt-in, that would be 500 contacts (let's say you collect their email address only this time). If you make sales by automation(automated email sequence) and sell to 2% of your 500 person list, you would have made 10 sales. If you took the value of the customers annually ($960) and multiplied it by 10 sales, you would have made, $9,600 automated, assuming customers stayed the entire year. That is only making 10 sales per year out of 10,000 followers. That is a .001% conversion rate from followers to customers. Your original investment was $5,000 to acquire customers and your gross revenue was $9,600. So you would have had a 1:2 input-output formula.

If you scaled up and invested $50,000 for 100,000 followers, how many sales would you make at a .001% conversion rate from followers to customers? You would have made 100 sales.

100 sales x $960 (annual value of a customer) = $96,000

Note: This example is for illustration purposes only. Results not guaranteed.

The illustrations above shows you the difference between converting manually vs automated. However, we can't forget those enrolled via automation can still be eligible for upsells that you may have to offer them. In fact, upselling the automated client is what most marketers do in order to generate more profits. Since the client has already made the commitment to purchase, there is a lower level of resistance to upgrade them into another service that will be able to serve them in a greater capacity.

Depending on the stage of your business, along with your personality type, you will have to determine whether or not you desire to make sales manually or automated. If you are just starting, I believe in closing in deals manually for the highest chance of growth and conversion. It may be pricy upfront; however, if you can figure out your input-output ratio, it can be extremely profitable.

Take a Moment

- **How much do you make per sale in your business? (Include upgrades if the customer enrolls into other products or programs.)**

- **How many customers must you acquire to reach your financial goals annually?**

- **What is the max budget that you are willing to spend to acquire customers and make a profit?**

- How many followers would you like to grow by in the next year?

- If you could develop a highly profitable ratio, how would that change your life?

Misconceptions about Ads

Although it's very enticing to imagine ourselves acquiring a world of followers, it's a more crowded space than it once was. Individuals, organizations, and businesses are packing the space with advertising, so it takes a bit more to catch a potential follower now. So how do you rise above the crowd in a noisy space?

I put together seven ways you can improve results with your ads to stand above the crowd, attract more followers, and encourage them to take action.

1. The Loss Leader Strategy

The loss leader strategy is when you give something of value away on the front-end for free; you know that you are losing up front, so that you can develop greater trust and credibility, which makes the sale easier on the back-end.

Maybe you have seen this strategy with cars sales before. You might have seen an ad for a new car at an extremely low cost. Since the car is at such a great price, you rush down to the dealership in the hope of buying it. By the time you get down there, it's already gone. So the salesman walks with you around the lot to look at the other cars that are available at the regular price point. At the end of the day, you go home with a car that is several thousand dollars more than what you wanted to spend. The car in the first ad served as the "loss leader," because the dealership took a loss by giving up their profit margin for that first car in order to attract more potential customers.

In social media, this concept is applied when you pay to run an ad that says you are giving away your product or service for free in the hopes of getting net customers after the offer has expired. It's human nature to avoid a loss up front if you can prevent it. However, does it really cost you? If you can have a great offer up front in order to attract customers that you never would have had otherwise, then why not offer a great value up front so you can win in the back-end?

2. Partnerships Are Powerful

You can find others who have a big following and have them promote you. This is one of the fastest ways to build an audience. If you can find someone who has the target audience you desire, you can connect with them. Sometimes they may recommend you to their audience. Your info may stay on their page per hour, per day, or as long as a week depending on what you are willing to pay them. It's a great investment, because they have worked really hard to build their list. Not only do you get access to their following, but you also have a higher level of credibility because they are referring to you as someone who is a qualified professional at what you do. If you are able to find a total of ten partners and acquire 1,000 new followers from each, you will have acquired 10,000 new followers. If you can convert 1% into sales, then you would have 100 new sales.

Note: This example is for illustration purposes only. Results are not guaranteed.

3. People Take More Action When There Is a Good Value Proposition

The idea to give something of value up front, in exchange for the purchase of something else—this is a value proposition. You are proposing that a customer should buy from you because of the additional value that you will provide to them as a customer. This value may include additional products or a service that they may get for free in addition to their purchase. If your goal is to gain them as a follower on your page, you may offer them a free survey, eBook, or a sample of your product if they follow you or opt-in to your email list. This is a great way to stand out from the crowd, because people like to buy something when they are getting a deal.

4. People Like People and Brands They Are Familiar With

If you can continue to promote ads to a specific target audience, those people will continuously see you. If the time is right, they will feel more comfortable to look into what you have to offer. If you are an individual, you can even create posts that promote who you are in order to boost face recognition and personal website branding. Remember, persistence lowers the viewers' resistance. That is often why big companies spend millions of dollars in advertising. They understand that if they are out of your sight, they are out of your mind. Social media advertising is a great way to stay in front of your audience until it's time for them to buy from you.

5. Work On Your Bold Promise

People often are curious when you offer a bold solution that can help them solve a problem they have. If you are able to articulate a solution that may benefit them in a big way, it may successfully convince your audience to take action. Your bold solution serves as a great trigger.

6. You Can Have Your Friends and Clients Leave Positive Feedback on Your Ad (Depending on the type of Ad)

When people read good reviews, they often think you must be credible at what you do. It can sometime ease the objections of the ad viewer—if the reviews they leave are genuine and positive. I recommend temporarily doing this until you are able to generate a real following of people that can promote positive feedback on your ads without you having to ask them to.

7. Create Viral Content and Utilize Free Advertising

Create the kind of content that studies have proven to go viral. This could include—videos of pranks, challenges, spoken word pieces, funny videos, creative and expressive videos, inspirational and motivational videos, and content that is informative and educational. People love things that add value to their life. They will often share it and give you free advertising.

Three things to NEVER do when you promote an ad:

1. Never Be "Salesy"

People don't like to be sold. They like to feel as though they are the ones in control of their buying decision. That is why the best promotions are often the ones that don't look like promotions at all. It's human nature to resist those ads we are not familiar with. This resistance occurs especially when the pitch comes right away, without building any trust first. It causes the buyer to question if your motives are to sell or to serve. Since there is low trust when an ad is pitching up front, people often will avoid that product or service.

2. When You Post an Ad, People Don't Like a Bluff

The majority of people don't waste their time clicking on a promise that is unrealistic. For example, "Lose thirty pounds in three days" and "Learn how to travel the world for free" don't seem feasible. Even if they could potentially be true, it's important not to make a promise that may cause the viewer to be extremely skeptical. People have internal radars that guide them away from marketers that make outrageous claims, and they tend to stay away from them. Instead, it's best to have a promise that is specific, direct, realistic, and attainable.

The only exception is if you have a lot of social proof that can validate your results to be true. You would need a lot of testimonials and corroborated evidence if you desire to make a bold claim on your ads.

3. **Never Place an Ad that Leaves Your Audience Confused about the Service or Product You Provide**

People don't like to waste their time with things that will not provide the information they are looking for. So if the front-end of the ad is a bold promise, the back-end of the ad should deliver.

For example, I was scrolling through my newsfeed one day when I came across an ad that said, "The best CRM system has now been released. Click here!" When I clicked on the ad, a video popped up. It was a two-minute long video that was full of great cinematography, but no content. Underneath the video in the comments people posted things like, "This ad completely wasted two minutes of my life." Another person wrote, "This was the most pointless ad I have ever seen." This sort of negative feedback makes it difficult to sell your product or service. For this reason, you want to make sure that you are clear about the specific outcome you can provide with your product or service.

Take a Moment

- **What were "aha!" moments in this chapter that you believe will help you in your promotions?**

- **How can you rise above the crowd when you promote online?**

- **If you were able to convert your following into customers, how would that make you feel?**

Sometimes people become attached to how they run their business and miss the most important part—FREEDOM! The whole idea behind promoting to an audience is so you can have leverage in your life and business. So many businesses stress over having to find new customers, but it doesn't have to be that way anymore.

There is a learning curve just like anything else. I believe you have a product or service that will impact people's lives, or you wouldn't be going through the process to learn how to reach more people online. Leaders know it's important to make sales, because that translates into helping someone with the resources you have been given. Sales is not only about making profits to help sustain your business and lifestyle, it's about giving people the things that will help make their lives and businesses more efficient. Remember that leaders rise above the rest. Don't compromise by aiming for the sale up front. Create real value and relationships with your following. I want to encourage you design your system flow thoroughly. Figure out your sales process and determine your input to output ratios.

STRATEGY FOUR

Leaders Partner with Influencers

*"You can spend years developing a following
or you can find an influencer that will promote
you to their following .*

— Adam Flores

It's no secret that the best form of business comes from referral marketing. The only challenge with relying on a referral is that you can't scale a business waiting on your friends to recommend you. Not to mention, you often will end up giving away hefty referral fee's to keep the referrals coming in the future if you are anything like me.

In search of a more predictable form of marketing, I was able to discover gold through the power of Influencer Marketing. Influencer marketing is about finding people who have built a trusted following online. They have been nurturing the relationship with their audience for years and have a trust and connection with their following.

What's most fascinating is the targeted reach and speed you get when an influencer promotes your content to their following. Not only do you find great engagement if your promotional content is relevant, you will find a massive amount of traffic to your offer rather quickly (An **offer** in this example refers to entry point at which someone has the ability to purchase a product or service from you). So how do you find these influencers? Well first it's important to understand the different types of influencers and what influencer marketing strategy will be best for you.

The first type of influencer is one who has built a following around a niche topic in order to attract the audience around that specific topic. The page is often built with the intention of advertising. If you find an influencer profile looking to promote, they will often mention the advertising option somewhere on the description of the page. I call this type of influencer a **featured account influencer**. They don't have a face behind the brand; instead, the following is being built based off the interest of a given topic. For example, a page may promote motivational business quotes to attract those interested in business inspiration. If you are the type of business that is looking for aspiring and existing entrepreneurs as your clients, this may be a good influencer to partner with.

Although they have a very large list of followers, the reality is that these aren't always the best form of influencers to partner with. However, it's the least barrier of resistance and can still get you a large, global, and targeted reach fast! At the end of the day, working with this type of influencer can still bring in a lucrative return. One thing you may want to be sure of is that the page the influencer is running has a pure level of engagement. If you aren't careful some of these profiles may have purchased fake followers and even buy fake engagement so that it looks attractive to advertisers. Don't fall for the trap!

When you connect with influencers I recommend building a relationship. If they have a quality page, with real engagement, you will find yourself continuing to promote with them. The real treasure often lies behind the scenes. Many featured account influencers have connections with other influencers, maintain a database, or may even be open to running affiliate campaigns with you. I strongly recommend taking the time to nurture your relationships with them instead of aiming only for a promotional transaction. It's only a matter of time before you will need their service again. If you treat them right, they often will give you a great deal on the next "round about".

One of the best ways to approach an influencer is to compliment the characteristics of the page and let them know that you are interested in becoming a promotional partner with them. Next, ask if them if they would be open to partnering with you on a promotional post. If they seem to be open to it, ask for their promotional calendar and rates for a post share. I usually aim to purchase post shares in a bundle in order to get the most reach for the best ad price.

Next, you want to identify your objective. Do you want to promote a webinar, a video series, a book, a website? What ever you are aiming to promote, make sure you are able to track your results through tracking links so you can measure the effectiveness of the influencer's page in which you are running your promotion. (If you don't understand how to do this, you can connect with our team for support).

Once again, look at your "input vs output ratios" to make sure you are converting for a profit. If conversions are lower than expected, track the area that is breaking down and adjust your funnel before running your new promotion. For example, I had a great conversion rate to one my landing pages. However, my webinar wasn't converting well do to a weak call to action on my webinar. I had to strengthen my close on the webinar and then I was able to get the conversions I was aiming for. Once you get a converting process, find as many targeted influencers as you can and promote your offer as frequent as possible. If your conversions continue to stay strong, take your offer to the affiliate marketing community and you can have them promote your content and share commissions. It's a really quick way to reach tens of thousands of followers quickly.

The other types of influencers are known as **Personal Brand Influencers**. These are people who use their name as the value of the brand. These personally branded influencers have spent countless hours building rapport with their following, giving them free value to earn trust, and have often invested tens of thousands of dollars building and promoting their brand to grow their following.

So why would they be interested in promoting you to their followers? Well they're a few reasons why they may want to promote you. One of those reasons is that you may have a product or service the influencers following would really be interested in. For example, let's say an influencer's brand was about living a healthy lifestyle. In this illustration, you want the influencer to promote your healthy cookbook. Your cookbook would be a desire among those motivated to live a healthy lifestyle. Therefore, the influencer may find your product to be a great fit with their audience. However, it doesn't mean that you will get a free hand out. They usually will want a one-time payment for the promotion, or they will want to split revenue with you if the profit margin is high enough. A standard revenue share wit this model is usually between a twenty-five and fifty percent split.

The power behind this model is that you don't have to spend years building a following. You can borrow someone else's audience and leverage their existing database. You can't forget the backend residual effects of running a promotion with a personal brand influencer. You'll gain credibility with their audience quickly, you'll gain more trusted followers, people will become aware of what you offer, and they may upgrade to a greater level of service you may offer. I can't even tell you how many times people have personally reached out to me from a campaign I ran with another influencer. It's pretty cool to see the level of trust they have for you when they see you have been referred by an influencer they already trust and respect.

So how do you target them? Great question! Find someone who shares your ideal audience. Typically the personal brand influencer will have a gatekeeper. I recommend pitching the gatekeeper on the value that you feel your product or service could bring and how you see great revenue potential in having such a partnership. Be very clear on your intentions and make sure the value is articulated so the gatekeeper understands the benefit to the influencer. Sometimes they may not be interested because their promotional schedule is already full. What do you do then? Then the law of reciprocation must come into play. What can you do to promote the personal influencer's brand? You can run ads to one of their products and screenshot the ad to display your effort to help them. You can promote their page to your followers and tag them so they get notified. One of the ways I am using this strategy is to invite them to speak at my live event. The only rule is that they have to promote my event to their audience. So now there is an exchange of value. What if you don't have a life event to offer? You can ask them to be a guest on your podcast and leverage the interview as a way to share the influencer's brand with your audience. Get creative and find ways that will benefit them. If you stay persistent in adding value, you will find yourself developing powerful relationships. When the personal brand influencers partner with you, your reach and conversions can be huge!

The third type of influencer is the **journalist.** These journalist often blog for big companies. Many companies, such as the *Forbes*, aim to find blogs they can feature on their webpage. How does this process work? You write a blog and submit it to the team that oversees the blog section of the company. If your topic is what they are looking for, they will approve your blog and publish it to their site giving you massive reach to their audience network. It may take a few blogs in order to get one featured on the site, when you do get it published, watch out! The traffic generated from these blogs can be serious. Although the journalist may not directly promote your product, they may share your company story, personal story, or the content that is relevant to their brand. This will often drive traffic to your website and add subscribers to your list. The traffic generated from these partnerships can be great and it's also a fun feature of credibility you can leverage since you're being published with a major journalist. It's a little bit of legwork and worth the wait and persistence.

Then there is the **Celebrity Influencer.** If you don't run in the Hollywood circle, it can be one of the most challenging influencers to partner with. *Beats by Dre* did an incredible job leveraging celebrities to promote the famous headphones that became a global sensation. Part of the reason the brand exploded is that celebrities were only allowed to use them at first. If you were not a celebrity, you could not access the product. This created an exclusive perception of the brand and soon after the launch went public, the brand exploded! *Apple* then purchased *Beats by Dre* for over one billion dollars.

There is no question that celebrities have great influence when it comes to marketing new products. That is why you see major companies leveraging celebrity fame to promote their brands. However, there is stillroom for the start-up entrepreneur to leverage celebrity clout. *Pencils of Promise*, a non-profit organization that builds schools for kids in third world countries, has done a great job of partnering with celebrities to promote the message of their organization. Lewis Howes, a podcaster and online entrepreneur, started from scratch interviewing local success stories and now interviews famous celebrities with one of the top business podcast channels.

There is no formula to connect with celebrities other than persistence and a great purpose behind your product. If you include celebrity influencers as part of your marketing strategy, make sure to add patience to the menu. It can be a challenging task to get acknowledged for your idea at first. However, if you stay persistent, a celebrity partnership can pay off big!

Affiliate Partnerships

As you connect with influencers, many of them have the potential to become affiliate partners. An **Affiliate Partner** is when someone is willing to promote your products or service to their network in exchange for a percentage of the profit. This used to be a tedious process because of the technology required to track your promotions back the affiliate who referred the client. Now, software's have become available for the average person to use and it has completely simplified this process.

For example, let's say you connect with an affiliate by the name of John. John is willing to promote you to his fifty thousand subscribers. As an affiliate, John will receive a link from you that will allow him to create an affiliate account and login to his affiliate portal. The affiliate portal will have a custom link already set up for John at the very moment John creates an account. When John's subscribers click on that custom link he sends out to his list of subscribers, the link will forward to your website, landing page, or webinar registration form. Even if the person clicking on the link does not purchase at that moment, it will track their purchasing behavior over the next 30 days. If the product or service is purchased within that time period, John will receive his commissions. It's one of the most powerful ways to reach a target audience.

Let's take a moment and the numbers. If John has fifty thousand subscribers and ten percent click on the link, then a total of five thousand subscribers click on the link. Of the five thousand that clicked, thirty percent requested to watch a web presentation on your business. That means that fifteen hundred people are now registered to watch your live training. Out of the fifteen hundred that registered only forty percent actually show up on your web training. That means you would have six hundred people actually watch your web-class. At the end of your web-class you offer a program for five hundred dollars. Out of the six hundred attendees, only seven percent purchase from you. That means you would have made forty two sales! If you can multiply the price of your program and the amount of sales, you would have made a total of twenty one thousand dollars in sales. Remember, the affiliate will receive half of the commissions. Each of you will receive ten thousand five hundred dollars for the day. This is how millionaires are created in the online space.

Formula illustration:

50,000 Subscribers x 10% click-through rate = 5,000 clicks
5,000 x 30% web-class registration = 1500 Web-class registrants
1500 web-class registrants x 40% show up rate = 600 attendees
600 attendees x 7% Sales = 42 Sales
42 Sales x $500 program = $21,000
21,000 x 50% (John's Affiliate Commission) = $10,500 for John
$21,000 - $10,500 (John's commission) = $10,500 payout left for you to keep (for the day)

Note: This does not include the follow up sales for the 60% that missed the web-class.

Take A Moment:

- **What type of Influencer would be the most beneficial for your business or organization?**

- **If you connected with someone who was willing to promote you to 50,000 of their subscribers that are your ideal clients, do you have the systems in place to do so?**

- **If you do NOT have systems in place to leverage partnerships, what action steps can you take to position your business to scale?**

Influencer and Affiliate marketing are both a very power process that can help you radically scale your business. There is a slight learning curve when you get started if you aren't the type of person to figure things out quickly. If you aren't tech savvy, you can always contact our company for support to help you with the process or you can hire a contractor to implement it for you. However, there is extreme leverage in the ability to reach such a large audience in a short amount of time and make massive amounts of sales on automation. My greatest desire for you is to see your get your message and mission out to world.

STRATEGY FIVE

Leaders Build Teams

*"Get out of the mindset that you can do
this on your own"*

—Adam Flores

Online marketing can have a lot of moving parts such as content writing, photography, design, ad campaigns, integrations, video creation, and editing. How in the world can you manage all of this as one person? You have to get out of the mindset that you can do this all on your own. As a leader, you want to be able to stay focused on activities that are going to move your business forward. That is why "it's key" to build a good team that can help you with video, content production, photography, design, ad campaigns, and backend operations.

In Michael E. Gerber's book, *The E-Myth Revisited,* he tells a story of a woman who was in love with baking apple pies. Her friends told her she should start an apple pie business. So the woman takes her friends' advice and opens up a business making apple pies. Immediately, she is inundated having to deal with all of the daily operations of running a business. Before you know it, she no longer gets to bake, because she is busy maintaining other tasks of the business. The very thing she was passionate about… is the very thing that she became enslaved to.

This woman's story helps to show us why it's important to build your business in a way that allows you to focus on what you are passionate about. So many people try to go out and do it on their own, but they can't possibly reach their potential trying to wear all of the hats in their businesses or endeavors that they pursue. You must be able to identify key people and implement systems that can help you create leverage in your business. Without it, it's hard to enjoy life. If you don't delegate responsibilities, how in the world is there enough time in the day to run a business effectively without trading your life to do it?

This was a personal struggle of mine for many years. Instead of having a team in place to help me—I *was* the team. I would make phone calls to acquire new customers, take phone calls from existing customers, manage my social media, organize campaigns, and manage everyday tasks in my business—not to mention—balancing my health, relationships, and family. My mind felt like it was in a million different places. I had to think about what I had to do today, what I needed to plan for the week, what content I had to create, what products I needed to develop, who I needed to respond to, and who I should reach out to. I got into business for freedom, and I felt like a slave to the long list of tasks I had to tackle every day. I knew building a team and a system was the answer; however, I didn't know where to start.

A documentary on the legendary Mark Cuban changed it all for me. Mark started a company back in the 90's that was to be the first broadcasting network to video stream college sports online. He was an ambitious entrepreneur who had a vision to be a revolutionary leader in his industry. The only problem was that he couldn't do it on his own. He had to get a team together to help him fulfill this vision. At that time, Cuban couldn't even pay his staff fully with benefits and salaries. What he did have was the potential to produce a monetary value for his team if he could turn his idea into a reality. So he recruited a staff and told them that he could only pay them with tacos and soda. They would have to work with him for free, and in the end, they would either become millionaires together or walk away as friends. With that, his team went to work… A year later this company went public, and the stocks went through the roof! His entire staff all became millionaires, and the hours that were sacrificed paid off. If Mark had been too scared to ask for help, or didn't start due to the lack of resources… He couldn't have touched the lives he did at this season in his life! Mind you – it wasn't just the people he made millionaires—this included their families and friends as well. I want YOU to imagine how your message could make an impact to this world—to one person? to thousands –even millions? Think big!

We all have intellectual property and ideas that can bring serious value to the people around us if we turn those ideas into realities. Often times, we doubt the value of our ideas and the impact that we have the ability to make. Although it can be a scary, an uncertain journey, we can't let our fears stop us from building what we know we are capable of. The question is, how do we build a team of people around our ideas to help us reach the end goal?

Social media is more fun when you have a team working to promote you. It helps to be able to have your videos and content put together by people who are skilled in those areas. My wish is for you to put a team together that can help you with everything you could possibly need in order to turn your idea into a reality.

I understand that you might not be willing to invest the capital to pay others to manage your social accounts, or you may not have the capital to invest anything if you are new in business. For those reasons, I put together five ways you can build a winning team to help you with social media even if you are not in a position to pay your staff. That way, you can divert tasks to people who have the time and expertise to help you expand your business.

1.   Enroll Them into Your Vision and Mission

I believe the start to building a winning team, is to cast a vision of where you are going. You should be able to articulate the potential of the opportunity you are working on. People like to follow visionaries, or those leaders who know the direction they are going. To bring people on board, you can articulate the projected earnings and the potential of the company. If you can find a way to incorporate a deeper purpose behind your vision, it becomes even more compelling for others to work with you. People want to be a part of something that has potential and adds meaning, value, and purpose to their life.

I remember in the early days of my business, I liked to call a few people over to a friend's condo that overlooked the beach. With a white board and a marker, I would draw out the vision and mission of the company. I would then articulate the vision to other people in the room and show them where we needed help. If they couldn't do it, I would ask them all for a referral of someone who could help us. We would have these "vision days" regularly, and invite people over to see what we were working on. People began to join the team, and it wasn't long before we had to be selective with who we would allow to work with us.

Most people drift through life without any direction. When you can give them an opportunity to be a part of a community that will help them thrive, they are willing to serve—as long as there is a vision and purpose worth serving.

2. **Use Your Network around You**

So many times people try and do everything on their own when they don't have to, because there are people in their lives who can help them. Don't let pride stop you from asking for help. Sometimes it's the people closest to you that have solutions that can help you reach your goals. If no one around you has the skill set you need, maybe they can learn to contribute something simple that will free you up to do something else more important.

Make sure to utilize the people who are willing to help. I remember I had some people on my team who never had any specific skill sets, but because they were included in the team and felt appreciated—they referred us to amazing people who did have the skill sets we needed. You never know who someone may know, or what someone is capable of learning unless you give him or her the challenge. Sometimes, someone who is willing to help, is better than someone who has a skill-set but does not want to give you their time.

3.   Identify a Win-Win Opportunity

I remember when I was first building my team, I thought, *"I don't have money to pay them, and why would anyone work for free?"* I didn't have access to the capital to bring in a part-time or full-time staff, and I sure wasn't in any position to provide benefits or even overhead for a building where people could work. So I thought of the value others could have if they worked with me. I realized that I had over twenty thousand dollars invested in my education—in leadership, Internet marketing, social media, and digital products. So I offered to give a few local college students access to my resources as they proved themselves through their work ethic. I let them know that I had access to information from industry leaders, outlined the experience they would get…and how it would ultimately help them reach their goals and visions. It was a win-win.

What fascinated me were those teammates who were willing to work simply to get access to higher knowledge—they actually worked harder than the people I had paid on past projects. Young people want to get experience, to learn, and to be a part of exclusive groups where they can feel included and valuable. People often value access to associations and education even more than a paycheck. If I had paid them hourly, it may have devalued the position, because they would have felt that they were worth more than what I was willing to pay. Sometimes the environment and culture you create will attract some of your best volunteers until you are able to pay them when the company thrives.

As leaders you have so much to offer others. You have ideas, environments, resources, partnerships, and connections. You must find a way to best leverage your own resources.

4. Be the Center Point of Referrals

Leaders often fail to leverage their networks—and networks are so valuable! The relationships you have may produce good clients, or serve as business for someone else. Give people the opportunity to create projects for you. If the work or service they provide is good, you can provide them referrals to key people in your network. If you have a great service provided to you, you will usually share your experience with your network anyway. If you can be a good source of referrals, often new professionals will do projects for free or for a minimal cost in the hopes of getting business from your network. You can be a significant center point for referrals.

Several of my teammates have special niches. Some are videographers, photographers, Internet marketers, etc. Due to the size of my network, I let them develop projects for me. If the project has promise, I refer them to other people who could benefit from their service. I only commit to providing referrals to the people who have partnered with me. People appreciate my loyalty to them, and in turn they do a lot of projects for free. It's a partnership that pays off through referrals and access to my network.

5. Give Up a Piece of the Pie

There are unique partnerships that may be necessary to supply the rare skills you need to grow your business. If someone is already highly valuable at what they do, they will not work with you unless they are being paid handsomely or getting ownership in the company. You can compensate them by giving them a percentage of the revenue that is generated on per-project basis, or if you are starting a company, you can leave room for investors and partners.

I know my strengths as a leader flourish more in the visionary role. I love to interact with people and do things that make a direct impact. I don't thrive working on detailed projects that require hours of being in front of my computer. With this in mind, I partnered up with someone who could help me on the technical side of my business. He also has a valuable skill-set to add to the group, so it was worthwhile to share my revenue with a partner who could bring in more value to each venture than if I were to do it on my own.

The Power Team

People often think you need a huge staff in order to grow your business on social media. It's actually quite simple. You only need a core group of people who have specific skills that can help you. Everything else is on a per-project basis. My goal for you—is to develop these teams so that you can leverage your message, products, or services and focus on what is important to your business or organization.

Your core group should consist of:

Media Team (Video and Photography)

Your ability to upload content in a relevant, clean, and relatable way is highly reliant upon a videographer or photographer who knows what they are doing. As a business leader, you want to be able to focus on your content—not all of the technical aspects of video editing. Sometimes you can start with your own simple equipment at first until you are able to bring on a media professional who can help.

Database and Campaign Manager

It can be a tedious process to manage your contacts and run effective campaigns. Find someone who is good with customer relationship management systems, and have them deal with the back-end database processes. You can formulate the campaign, but let your teammate help you manage it and promote it to your audience.

Content Creator/Manager

Social media moves fast and it's nice to have someone that can create and distribute your content across all of the social platforms.

Copy Writer and Ads

Communication through creative writing is a powerful way to make sales online.

It's one of the harder positions to fill; however, finding a good copy writer who that can write copy, create ads, and manage your ads is a good role to fill.

Outside Resources

With technology consistently improving, you can also utilize software and apps to help you reach a larger audience faster. In my *Business Club Academy*, I go more in depth regarding the tools and resources that are good to use. Don't be afraid of technology; instead, use it to your advantage.

Everything else is usually on a per-project basis. For instance, you may need a graphic designer or web developer on occasion for special projects. My encouragement to you is—to not be intimidated by building a team. It's actually pretty straightforward and you can still do it with very low overhead. You may start by doing things on your own in the beginning, and that is okay, too. However, if you are running a large business, then you obviously would want to build a team of people who can help.

Take a Moment

- **Who in your network would be willing to master social media to help you grow your organization or business?**

- **How can you utilize the resources around you to benefit others in a way that is worth it for them and worth it for you?**

- **What creative ways can you offer value to others in return for their service to help you?**

Create a Winning Culture

As you begin to build a team, you must create a winning culture. Make sure that everyone is on the same page and operating on the same level. Everyone on the team should have a clear task and be fully aware of what they are to do in order to reach their goal. Find out what each member's strengths are and place those members in a position they will enjoy. People will work harder when they can thrive in an area in which they are already interested. It's your job as leaders to find that sweet spot.

John Wooden, former UCLA basketball coach, mastered this technique. He would design plays for each of his player's strengths. For example, if a player was good at making a shot in a particular spot on the court, Wooden would design a play that would allow that player to shoot from that sweet spot. Most coaches don't operate that way. Other coaches will typically run a play that is fundamental to the game of basketball. Although that strategy of "fundamentals" may be effective, it may not fit the specific players on the court. John Wooden's approach was special because of his ability to maximize the potential of each individual player.

As leaders, it's your job to keep up the morale of the team. You need to be able to recognize those who are working hard and celebrate the little successes along the way. When you have fun and create a culture that is innovative and rewarding, people tend to give their best work. You don't need a base of operations like Google in order to get others to be creative and work hard. Although it would be nice, it's not necessary to bring about great results. Just think, Apple's first office was in a garage. You can start anywhere as long as you and your team are working together towards a common goal. You can do it on your own, but leaders usually choose to involve others; it's more fun that way.

Get Clarity

We have covered a lot of ground so far. I want to encourage you to clearly establish what you want your outcome to be. Start with your vision and work your way backwards to daily tasks that need to be implemented in order to reach your goals. Find people who can help you with those tasks so that you can stay focused on what you are good at. Don't let the thought of having to do everything on your own intimidate you. It will take time to find the right people; however, I want you to know that there are people out there who have the missing pieces of the puzzle. Keep your eyes open. The goal is to build a system and a team that are able to help you grow your business so you can have the freedom to do what you love. One of the best feelings is when your business or organization is reaching an audience even when you are not there.

STRATEGY SIX

Leaders Start Movements

*"If you want to start a movement,
give people a cause worth sharing."*

—Adam Flores

If you want to reach the pinnacle of success on social media, one of the highest levels of influence is when you start a movement. As leaders, you have the ability to start something bigger than yourself. In order to do so… you have to identify a cause that is greater than yourself and get others engaged in it. If the right cause is in place and you have provided the right tools, you may find an army of people sharing your message.

Could you imagine if you led a viral movement through social media? What would it look like? There is power when others unite together and spread a message on your behalf to an audience who knows them and trusts them. I've spent many of my years studying movements. My attraction to this area of study has come from my heartfelt belief in people and my sincere desire to see change in a broken world. I have always had this strong yearning within me to see people get the most out of life. I know it might seem cliché, but if I could build a whole community of people who wanted to win in life and business, I could make a difference for a lot more people than I ever could on my own. That's where I got the drive to start my first movement online that exponentially expanded my business. Not only was it extremely rewarding financially, it added a lot of meaning to my life. Having a group or community follow your cause is one of the most powerful ways to promote what you do. People will follow you if you have vision; they will sacrifice everything for the right cause. In a world full of challenges, movements are necessary catalysts for positive change. People are looking for someone to lead a new movement right now, and I hope this chapter convinces you that the next movement could be yours.

You may feel like you don't have the personality, skills, or leadership ability to start a movement. Although, bear in mind that people who have the highest social and economic statuses are typically not the ones to start movements. Mother Teresa was a great example. She built a following of missionaries to take care of the poor and sick when she couldn't be there to tend to them herself. She made a tremendous impact in her lifetime, and had very little political power and resources to start with. She was determined to make a difference, and stood up for a cause that was worth fighting for. Martin Luther King, Jr. was also a great example of someone who came from humble beginnings. He started the Civil Rights Movement, which was one of the largest movements in history! Although he was a pastor and human rights activist with an amazing gift as an orator, he still lacked power to make a difference on his own. His passion to fight for the betterment of humanity — inspired an army of supporters to help bring about change.

If you show me a movement, I'll show you the great idea that helped bring about its influential change. People think that ideas are what attract people, but the true magnetism is the passion behind the idea — something compelling! You don't have to be a powerful, persuasive, or an articulate speaker, but you do need an idea that compels people to follow you. One of the greatest examples of this is Moses. In the Old Testament, God tells Moses to lead the Israelites across the Red Sea. Moses doesn't believe he is very well-spoken… at least not well enough to lead the people. So as the story goes…Moses asks God to send his brother, Aaron because he is a better speaker. God didn't want to delegate the mission to Aaron who was more capable. Instead, he deliberately told Moses to go, and ensured Moses that He would be with him. Moses went on to lead a movement of people and free the Israelites from the slavery of Pharaoh, despite his lack of confidence in himself.

I share that story because if you feel called to start something, don't let fear stop you. Every leader has his or her doubts, because with a great vision, there is always resistance. Let go of the burden of having to save the world. People often feel a movement needs to be tens of thousands of people in order for it to work. But if you're starting a movement that truly impacts others and makes a difference, then even if your impact only reaches a few- -its worth it. You don't have to lead hundreds of thousands of people for you to consider yourself the leader of a movement (although you can do that, too). Even local movements can be great forces for growth and change. Whether it is a big movement or a small movement, it will still take courage. You need to have guts to stand for what you believe in—when at first—you're the only one. It takes courage to declare that change should be made, especially when no one is following you. It takes a leap of faith that the ideas behind the vision will actually come to fruition and that a difference will be made. Rallying people together and reminding them of your vision demands hard work. People are afraid that it might not work, and that is often why they never start. At the end of the day, a leader doesn't want to possibly damage his or her ego if the movement doesn't take off. In reality, the only reason you could fail in starting a movement is if that movement is about you! Keep your focus on the vision and the solution you are bringing to the world.

How does all of this relate to the social media side of business? Social media connects us globally. Businesses and organizations that have started movements online have had tremendous success. Many businesses never start a movement simply because they don't understand how it can turn into a profitable venture. Take a look at the five ways movements can radically enhance your business or organization.

Movements in Business Bring:

1. Loyalty and Commitment

Everyone wants to be a part of something bigger than they are—have a sense of purpose. Movements give people the opportunity to link arms with others who are like-minded. A collaboration of efforts toward a common cause creates a group identity, or culture, where people feel a sense of belonging. If a group of people supports the same cause, those people carry a level of responsibility to help the movement move forward. People will work harder for others than they will for themselves. You will seldom find someone who lets another person down—especially when there is a great cause behind their efforts. Also, in a movement, there is greater retention within the customer base, because people are emotionally connected to the purpose behind the movement. This commitment prevents losing customers to competitors, and creates reoccurring purchases for other products the brand may offer. Starting a movement breed's loyalty, which translates into reoccurring revenue.

Apple is a great example of this process. There are several competitive communication and technology companies around the world, but what made Apple so successful? Other than its amazing technology, it has been the dominating company in developing a movement behind their products. If you have ever watched a video made by Apple, they're always sharing the reasons why they create their products. Every product released is packaged with a message behind it. These messages are compelling and sell Apple's vision, which is why the company has created such strong loyalty with its users. This didn't happen by accident. Apple has created a community to champion their products; they make people feel like they are a part of their new discoveries that change the world. It's a movement that has reached all corners of the globe—which is why Apple continues to be a dominating company in technology and communications.

What we learn from Apple is that it's possible to build loyalty in this day and age among our customers—even when competition is fierce! The right messaging makes a difference, and a compelling vision entices people to become a part of the journey. Your videos, can have an incredible impact that utilizes a compelling message to engage your customers. When you can touch the emotional side of the viewer, you'd be surprised by the effect it can have on someone.

2. The Highest Quality Referrals

The reason people join a movement is often because someone shared a compelling reasons for them to be apart of it. TOMS® shoes company is a great example of this. TOMS® started the *One for One* movement: For every one pair of shoes purchased from TOMS®, they donated a pair of shoes to kids in need. Thanks to social media, this program became a viral movement due to the rapid shares online and offline. People began to spread the word and share this beautiful cause. They would explain how they are helping a child somewhere in the world—promoting it to their friends and followings because it gives them a sense of significance and/or purpose. TOMS' ® social sites gained millions of followers—raising their voices to collaborate and spread the movement.

If someone is willing to share a captivating purchase experience, it will often encourage another person to become apart of the experience and purchase the same product or service. This type of referral creates a compound effect. One person communicates the message to another person who shares the same message. People are more likely to buy something or join a movement for a *cause* that drives them — rather than just buy a product or service alone. Therefore the highest quality referrals come from those who share the passion behind their product or service.

3. **Excitement, Momentum, and Attention**

People use social media to garner awareness about movements that create rapid change. We love to see results produced quickly when we put effort behind something we believe wholeheartedly in. Those people who get involved in the exponential effects of a movement create momentum that can bring in unprecedented results. Positive results then boost the morale of the people working with you, increase the excitement of people who are involved, and attract attention for the people yet to become involved.

You can find a great example of what this looks like in the nutrition industry. Many health and fitness companies release a "90 Day Weight Loss Challenge" in the hopes of bringing rapid awareness to their product line. People share photos of their "before-and-after" results on their social sites. Due to the massive number of positive results being shared on some of these sites, people become intrigued by the excitement and results—this often leads people to inquire about the product line. The movement to be fit is creating a lot of momentum for nutrition companies, and it's attracting a lot of attention for the products that are being used to help people reach their fitness goals.

As a leader, it's your job to show people what is possible. How can you utilize results in your movement to bring rapid awareness to your audience on social media? If you can find a way to do so, you will see more excitement among your business partners and followers, you will attract more attention to your brand, and peak the curiosity of people who would have never been interested otherwise.

4. A Community and a Culture that Gives People a Voice

Movements bring people together due to the commonality of a unique and specific purpose. This unity can serve to create a culture and community where they can feel connected. Ideas are exchanged — giving people a place to share their opinions and express how they feel. This interaction and engagement are great for strengthening relationships within the group, as well as, attracting attention from people who may not yet be involved. People want to be a part of a community and a culture that allows them to share their experiences. They will often do more than what is asked of them simply for the benefit of the group and the cause. This selflessness promotes greater productivity, and can lead to considerable progress toward the end goal — GoPro is a great example of this.

There are several other HD video cameras in today's market place, so how is it that GoPro has been able to dominate the HD video space for the outdoors? What separates GoPro from the rest? It has created a diverse community of people who film anything from extreme sports to their baby's first steps, and that has brought in massive awareness to their brand! GoPro is promoted by their consumers' experiences, and they have given people a chance to express themselves, via selfie video, underwater experience, or extreme adventure, to their own audience by utilizing their HD cameras. It's a movement that has become so strong, that it has formed its own community.

As a business owner, or one in-the-making… the secret to gaining momentum within your business is to give your followers a sense of ownership in your company. People who feel so connected to someone's business, feels free to express their love for the product or ideals that it has. I believe you can gain power and influence when you include their opinions about new up and coming products, ideas, or concepts which in turn makes them feel like they're friends with the CEO or President of the company. One great example of this is the political campaign trail… The candidates have their own Facebook account and email addresses where they share ideas. Through these venues, the candidates gather the information their followers give, thank them, and at times use these suggestions vocally during their rally's – thanking the followers again! This creates a sense of ownership on their fan base, because their ideas were heard! Who doesn't want to be noticed by the potential President?

5. **New Revenue**

    Traditional ways of marketing such as, flyers, running ads in the paper, making posters, etc… can take some time to develop revenue due to the process of exposing people to the service, product, or concept that doesn't reach out to very many people at once. There was a time when brick and morter stores relied heavily on 'word of mouth' in order to advertise… Now, these same stores in just a few seconds can send an ad out to an entire community in seconds on social media! Social media allows for movements to accelerate the process and promotion at an unprecedented rate!

    A great example of the new revenue potential that can be generated online is The Ice Bucket Challenge. The Ice Bucket Challenge was one of the most viral fundraising campaigns ever created on social media. It produced forty times the fundraising amount for ALS than the year prior, raising tens of millions of dollars. It consisted of people videotaping themselves dumping a freezing cold bucket of ice water over the top of their heads, and challenging three friends to donate to the cause and do the same thing. The purpose was to bring awareness to ALSA.org (a nonprofit that supports research and helps patients who suffer from problems with their nerve and cell disease). There were millions of videos uploaded on this challenge, and it changed the way non-profits value the use of raising funds through the social space. It was a massive way to reach an audience for a great cause.

As leaders, sometimes you need to be able to generate funds quickly to help the people you aim to serve. You need funds to sustain your message, promote your products or services, and give back to those in need. In what ways can you start a movement on social media to generate awareness quickly?

Leaders - Who Start Movements... Leave Clues

If you look at some of the greatest movements of all time, many times you would observe a radical leader who led people to fight for a cause. The purpose, the fight for change, often serves as the driving force for people to stay committed until the end goal is reached. Although you don't need to put your life on the line to start a movement on social media, you still need to identify what moves large amounts of people to take massive action.

Success leaves clues. I believe if you can take some of the principles from great leaders before us, and apply these principles in the online world, you can make a difference and a fortune. Every movement starts with one—that one person with an idea and the courage to lead from the front. It takes a person of vision and burning desire to reach a goal. In order to start a movement, you must have a driving force. There are different visions and goals that we aim for as people. We can aim to acquire money, items, experiences, accomplishments, and even greatness. Although those are great motivators, nothing moves people more than a purpose to make a difference. For that reason, you need to be able to tap into a deeper purpose within yourselves and within your business. As business owners or leaders of an organization, there has to be something you can fight for other than money itself. If you can identify a compelling reason behind how you can enhance the lives of others, it can serve as a driving force—giving you energy, passion, and a deeper meaning to life. You want to identify a clear and irresistible reason, so that others feel empowered to enroll in your vision and mission.

Take a Moment

- **How can your products or services be used to change lives or solve an injustice in the world?**

- **What cause are you fighting for?**

Starting a movement doesn't have to be this intense push to change the world; it actually can be very simple. It's very similar to the steps I covered to promote your business on social media. The major difference is that you are incorporating purpose into a movement and are leading with a cause instead of focusing on the product or service first. You are also working to build a community of loyal and vocal fans who will champion your message on your behalf so that you can reach people faster.

You'd be surprised how quickly the word can spread. I remember releasing my first content videos when I launched my movement, and it reached tens of thousands of people due to all of the shares it accrued. I had business flowed unlike anything I've ever seen before, and it didn't require as much involvement as I originally imagined. A movement is comprised of a lot of people carrying out social change a little at a time. Utilizing social media creatively can mean massive profits depending on the business model or organization. However, the leader needs to start it and lead with the right message.

Leaders Need a Plan

As a coach, I have a lot of people who come to me with different ideas. Almost everyone has a vision, but fewer have a mission, and hardly anyone has an effective plan drawn out. It's not enough to have a vision without a plan; it's like having a car without gas. It's important to have a road map on how to execute the plan of action in order to fulfill the vision and the mission—this that way, it is clear to everyone involved. For those of you with a clear vision and mission… I challenge you to create a plan! I'm going to give you the framework for you to follow that has helped many businesses—including my own—start a movement online.

Seven Steps to Start a Movement on Social Media

1. Develop an Identity

People like to be a part of something that is established and in place. For that reason, you should develop a name and motto for your movement along with a vision and mission statement; stating what you wish to accomplish. It should be short and self-explanatory. Work with graphic designers to get logos, banners, or creative digital graphics on your page. If you plan to make any flyers or t-shirts, they can also help serve as promotional tools as people begin to get involved.

Determine the social media platform you will be using. If you are on several different platforms, it may help to start on the platform where you have the most connections. Create a group with its own page, upload videos, and post content that describes what the movement is about. This page should include an area for interactive comments. Figure out the story you want to tell. You should be able to articulate your cause. Then, identify the emotional angle that will engage the followers that will be added to your group.

You should also have a stand-alone website with an opt-in page. You can post the link to your website on all of your social media pages so you can be in position to grow a list of people. That way, you can follow up on the back-end. It serves as another way to communicate with your following if you launch campaigns in the future.

Include any professionals or influential people in your group or on your page, and begin to invite your network to join the group or page. You can send out personalized messages that emphasize the importance of your cause. Begin with posts that may include interactive comments, or debatable topics in order to spark engagement with new followers.

Don't hesitate to promote and build your movement offline as well. People who you meet offline have social sites, and can still help spread the message to their audiences.

2. Rally the Troops

Begin to share your ideas among people who you feel would be good partners in assisting you with the movement. Identify people who are committed to linking arms with you and helping you with your cause. Typically in the group, there will be some people who are more interested and involved than others. Strengthen your relationships with those people, and find whatever skills or gifts they have that can help contribute to the group on a greater level.

Look for people that can help you fulfill the plans you have drawn out. Among your followers, you may find—graphic designers, media professionals, marketers, etc. Give them the opportunity to take on a project to help support the cause. You can also encourage your most influential leaders to recruit other people to be a part of the group—people who may add a specific value that the group needs.

Make sure everyone on the team is fully aware and enrolled in the vision and mission. You should nurture your first followers as equals, which will show them that the movement is not about you. If your followers see a self-serving plan to reach the masses then your movement will likely have no significant impact.

3. Run Your Campaigns

Define the goals and outcomes of your campaign. Build pages that will help promote and support the community you wish to establish. Form groups for members where you can communicate in private with each other. Run ad campaigns and promote your cause. If you have a staff or loyal followers, engage them in the proliferation of the movement. Your staff can serve as a great voice to spread the message. Be sure you are clear on the action steps you wish for followers to take. You want to be able to influence key decision makers. It's important that, as the leader, you are not always the one who is promoting the message. You want your followers to take ownership of that same message, too.

4. Share Common Concerns

Share common concerns that can potentially engage like-minded people who can join in and support your cause. You should post content that displays the problems you wish to eliminate as a movement. The audience should be clear as to why the problems are directly affecting people, the environment, animals, etc. People need to be able to empathize and relate on a human level.

Although you want to bring awareness to the problem, it's also important to be focused on the solution. You don't want to create an environment that gives off a negative energy. People should be comfortable expressing their desires and visions for a solution. To help establish this atmosphere, you can develop content that addresses the changes you wish to see.

Your environment and community of people will be shaped by the content you post and the way you represent your movement. Find a way to emotionally express the value of your movement, casting the vision, and the mission to your audience and –expressing how you can work together to fulfill your goals. Stories and testimonials are a powerful resource. You should make sure that the stories you tell are captivating and engaging—that they pull at the heart of your audience and inspire them to get involved. Let others give their feedback, and let your followers become your voice.

5. Utilize the Right Social Media Strategies

Work on your positioning and utilize the right tools that can help generate a following around your cause. It's vital that you use a social platform that gives people the flexibility to express what the cause means to them. They should be able to share videos or written responses. You can even use apps and other creative tools to strengthen communication within the group.

Be creative in your delivery. Create challenges, make viral videos, and create content that can be shared by your following. It helps to know what is trending in the media, and then use it as a tool to bring awareness to your brand or organization.

You can also utilize social media to promote events. You can rally your followers together and have meetings offline. This helps tighten your community and can serve as a great way to get others involved.

6. Recognize Others

You can inject humor and fun in your organization or business through the videos and posts you create. Sometimes starting a movement can feel like a serious business, but it shouldn't always be like that. Give shout-outs and offer prizes to those who are contributing the most to promotion efforts. People like to be recognized and feel special.

Discover roles for the dedicated partners, group members, and followers, and get them engaged to serve in a more structured and committed way. People may not always take on more responsibility on their own, but they love to be asked and appreciated.

7. **Measure Your Results**

Work on your system flow and see what you can improve to turn your following into customers and profits for your business or organization. Look at your growth and figure out what is working. Run different campaigns and see what engages your following the most. Challenge the team to discover creative ways to reach more people, and tighten the system that converts them. You should continuously fine-tune your system for an optimal response.

Never forget to share successes with the team, as well. Make sure you are responsive with stories that let them know how the movement is making an impact. When results are produced, and you can see even the smallest difference that the whole team made together, you should celebrate and share the results with your audience. People love to contribute to something that is moving and making an impact.

Developing Leadership Within

If you have ever seen a raindrop fall on top of a flower, it is a beautiful sight, as unique as a diamond. The only reason it's not valued like a diamond is because it doesn't last. In the same way, there are a lot of attractive businesses in the online space. However, many of them don't last because they are after quick success.

Leaders build things that last and that make a difference. If you want to be a leader, you must understand that great things come over time, not overnight. It takes time to learn in general, and it takes even more time to try—fail—and learn from the mistakes you make along the way; that is how you develop experience. The challenges you face enhance your character and help you gain a better understanding of yourself and what you can do.

If you haven't yet noticed, starting a movement and reaching an audience is the "people business." That is why it's essential that you invest in your leadership skills as well as work on your social media skills. You want to keep the "edge on" technology while applying wisdom and insight that helps you win with people. You can't only work on your business—you must also work on yourself. If you can spend time strengthening your leadership qualities, and it can transfer into ideas that you can bring into the online space; you will end up rising above the crowd every time. Leaders who lead to make an impact will always have a space in the online world. You have a unique opportunity to make your mark!

Starting a movement is a great way to make an impact beyond your own abilities. Although movements increase financial gain in your businesses and organizations...they also add more meaning to your work as you move towards your goals. They create excitement to do something big and enable you to collaborate with like-minded people who can join you on the journey.

Movements empower us all to live for a purpose. My desire is to see you put a plan together to start one. I believe you have a gift and can provide solutions to the world—People are waiting for you!

STRATEGY SEVEN

Leaders Focus On Impact

"The true measure of a person's heart is their willingness to serve those who can do nothing for them."

—Adam Flores

The people I find who are attracted to a book like this are usually the ones looking to live their lives with a greater sense of purpose. If you made it this far in my book, then you are probably one of those people. If so, you want to learn the skill sets necessary to succeed in your field so that you can serve others and make a greater impact.

In my experience, life is best lived when serving others. In fact, I would argue that the true measure of a person's heart is their willingness to serve those who can do nothing for them.

Leading with a heart drawn to service allows us to be pulled toward our destiny. People are desperate to follow true leaders who really care. Although leaders should be programmed to *give*, it's always amazing when we get the opportunity to receive. I have opened many life-changing thank you cards from people who I have personally touched, and my inbox is full of messages from people who have been inspired by the content I post. It's incredibly fulfilling to know that my message and story inspires others. My hope is that by now, you may have some clarity on who it is you wish to help and how you can reach them. It's one of the greatest rewards when you can build an audience around what you love.

Sometimes it helps to take a break from your busy life and rest in silence—allowing yourself time to discover the true meaning behind your life experiences. One of the mightiest forces of human nature is when you realize the power of your dream and how it can impact people in a profound way. When you understand how your story and life experiences can make a difference, you feel obligated to go out and share it with the world. Obligation seems to be a common characteristic among those who give back in this social space. The people who often make the greatest impact—are those who feel they have a great gift that they can't help but share it with others.

I hope this book has served to help you position and market yourself in a way that gives you the confidence and courage you need to reach your target audience. Not only do I hope that this book gave you the confidence to share your message, I hope it helped to equip you with the skills you need to start making your fortune.

Sometimes, it can be a touchy subject to discuss making a lucrative income and giving back at the same time. Thanks to my associations and my faith, my perception of money began to change, and I began to see it as a tool. If someone offers to pay you for your help in a particular area, don't turn it down. Learn to receive money as something that can help you reach more people. It's an amazing resource, and I want you to be comfortable talking about it. The world often portrays rich people as evil and poor people as righteous. Just think back to movies you have watched; isn't it hard to think of a movie where the rich guy is the good guy or the hero? Many times we are programmed to shy away from the notion that wealthy, benevolent people actually exist. In fact, many of my circles of friends are very well-off, and they are some of the best people I know. It's not the money that defines you; it's your character that defines you. If you have good morals and a friendly, generous personality, money will be put to good use in your hands, so you should accept it. In this space of social leadership, there are so many opportunities to get paid for what you do, so I encourage you to share your message and make as much as you can.

I would like to leave you with an uplifting passage I once wrote in my journal. One night, I felt inspired to become more innovative, and this passage came to me.

Whose Hands?

Have you ever realized that the value of something changes depending on whose hands it's in? For example, a baseball in my hands is worth five dollars. A baseball in Alex Rodriguez's hands is worth a thirty million dollar salary. But a basketball in my hands is just a game of horse. But a basketball in Michael Jordan's hands produced six NBA championships. A football in my hands is a game of two-hand touch. But a football in Joe Montana's hands is a touchdown pass to Jerry Rice and the birth of a legacy. It all depends on whose hands it's in. Just like a paintbrush in Michelangelo's hands or an idea in the mind of Steve Jobs, the value all depends on the hands that shape what they've been given. To the leaders, the creators, the innovators, and the people who want more out of life, we all have the ability to create something great with our hands. We can't let narrow minds limit us to what is possible. Since you are made in Gods hands, you are created as a masterpiece. You have gifts and abilities that God has given you. Since you are in the hands of greatness what will you create?

I remember looking out of the restaurant window of that second story of the golf shop where I used to work. I wondered how people were able to have the time and income to play golf every day, and I promised myself that I would figure it out and make a difference in the world. I was just a kid then, and some would argue that I am still a kid. But looking back on what I've accomplished since then, it's surreal to think how far I have come and the lives I have touched. With hard work and the right application of your vision, you could be in the same position sooner than you could imagine.

Someone in the world needs your message, your product, or your service, and thanks to social media, you now have hundreds of resources and connections at your disposal. So what else are you waiting for? Go out and share your passion with the world — they are waiting on you.

Made in the USA
San Bernardino, CA
15 December 2018